Exploring Boundaries

Exploring Boundaries
The Architecture of Wilkinson Eyre
Peter Davey, Kurt W. Forster

Birkhäuser
Basel · Boston · Berlin

Design and production: Jannuzzi Smith, London
(Michele Jannuzzi, Flavio Milani, Benoît Santiard,
Richard Smith)

Reprographics: DawkinsColour, London

Printing: Freiburger Graphische Betriebe, Freiburg im Breisgau

Bibliographic information published by Die Deutsche
Bibliothek. Die Deutsche Bibliothek lists this publication in
the Deutsche Nationalbibliografie; detailed bibliographic
data is available in the internet at http://dnb.ddb.de.

Library of Congress Control Number: 2007922516

© 2007 Birkhäuser Verlag AG
Basel · Boston · Berlin
P.O. Box 133, CH-4010 Basel, Switzerland

Part of Springer Science+Business Media

Printed on acid-free paper produced from chlorine-free pulp.
ECF ∞

Printed in Germany

ISBN 978-3-7643-7531-7

9 8 7 6 5 4 3 2 1

www.birkhauser.ch

Hulls Held Aloft and Bridges that Blink
Thoughts on the Architecture of Wilkinson Eyre
by Kurt W. Forster

[1] Pier Luigi Nervi, "Problemi dell'architetto," in: *Casabella*, vi (1933), 5, p. 34; reprinted in *Storia moderna dell'arte in Italia, III: Dal novcento ai dibattiti sulla figura e sul monumentale*, 1925–1945, ed. by Paola Barocchi. Turin: Einaudi, 1990, p. 302. Giulio Carlo Argan, in his early biographical sketch of the engineer, *Pier Luigi Nervi* [Milan: Il Balcone, 1955, p.10], argues that "Nervi considers . . . the method of his research to be intrinsically aesthetic."

[2] Nervi, in: *Casabella*, vi (1933), 5, p. 34: "Quello che e' fondamentale, per la concezione architettonica, e' la comprensione dello spirito del nostro tempo, di quel non so di dinamico, di deciso, di audace che ne pervade le manifestazioni intellettuali; e lo sfruttamento delle capacita' tecniche e industriali, considerate come meravigliosi strumenti per piu' meravigliose sinfonie."

Chris Wilkinson and Jim Eyre are architects whose practice defies the customary division between how a building is actually constructed and how it looks to the eye. They share with an earlier exponent of their approach, Italian architect Pier Luigi Nervi, the conviction that "for the very idea of architecture, an understanding of the spirit of the times" will prove indispensable, a grasp of "what is dynamic, decisive, and daring in its intellectual manifestations."[1] They might argue with Nervi that this is because "the works we build not only bear the traits of our age, they also mirror our spirit and our capacity whose enduring reflection and identity will be judged by future generations."[2] To be sure, Wilkinson Eyre have already been examined by their contemporaries and found to possess exceptional capacity to work in difficult situations and for diffident clients, such as railroad and municipal administrations. Moreover, their latest projects venture beyond the classic domains of structural engineering—industrial buildings, terminals, and bridges —and infrastructure, proposing instead museums, schools, office towers, and greenhouses.

With the latter, we return to some of the earliest explorations in metal-and-glass construction, which proved to be a powerful engine in the transformation of architecture during the last two centuries. On the vacant site of the nearly vanished Crystal Palace, the empty knoll in Sydenham where only the retaining walls of its base have been left in place, Wilkinson Eyre have proposed a new permanent structure. An elegant glass-clad capsule, the length of the original transverse aisle of the Palace, perches high above the site, offering visitors a spectacular view of the city. As a hovering "craft," the proposed capsule is imagined at the scale of the grandest dirigibles, carrying with it a memory of a now-distant time and a taste of our own space-age fixation on "capsules for survival." As a landmark visible from afar and

7

offering far-reaching views for visitors, this new crystal craft suggests a platform from which the imagination might take flight whilst keeping an eye on the city about to be left behind. The project balances contradictory impulses: a mock-up of the future which will instantly reduce the world to purely specular experience, and a reminiscence of the mid-19th century euphoria for mechanical invention. Hovering above the treetops and skirted by the ruined retaining walls of the Palace, Wilkinson Eyre's structure would add to London what the Millennium Dome could never achieve. The image of an "abandoned" platform below and an inexplicably suspended object in the sky has the power to recall one of the key images of the last century: Leonidov's dirigible tethered to a pyramid. Maximum stability and its opposite, levitation, form a pair of paradoxical antagonists. One is tempted to think of Wilkinson Eyre's work as a kind of meditation on these paradoxical states, a balancing act performed not just in the realm of the imagination, but among the forces of reality that are in play rather than at rest. Because Wilkinson Eyre really reflect on the paradox and imagine a structure that negotiates its own conflict, any echoes of Archigram and their capsules lumbering on pneumatic stilts across the territory of the city are faint, indeed. Not to speak of "elegance," on which we shall hear more from Gustave-Alexandre Eiffel, nor of landscape. Wilkinson Eyre are not taking up where the Crystal Palace left off, theirs is not a giant greenhouse, but an otherworldly hull that descends into nature rather than enshrining it.

The idea of a self-contained capsule made its appearance early in their work and is never completely out of view. It took shape in the Magna project, not just as a formal feature, but as a concept capable of assuming four fundamentally different states. In keeping with the project's purpose of illustrating the "history" of steel at a now idle site of steel-making, each

8

"pavilion," as the architects call them, houses one of the four ancient elements—earth, air, fire, and water. Below and above ground, the elements assume a different "historical" reality, their manifestation remaining palpable even if it issues from a cosmography now far removed from our own experience. Water takes the form of a steel-shaped wave, and air the hollow of its own displacement in the guise of a giant shell. The *container*, in one form or another, seems to come closest to Wilkinson Eyre's concept of space, a container, moreover, shaped by its own structural properties rather than external exigencies. Their space-capsules seem destined to capture and shelter what cannot float free or suffer exposure. As we are biologically limited beings in just such terms, the idea of the pod assumes vital relevance and anchors our imagination in our own genesis as human beings rather than in any of the abstractions so dear to the early years of modern architecture. It is not Cartesian abstraction or mechanical regularity that prevail in Wilkinson Eyre's work; instead they are always proposing containers-in-the-void. One does not need to enumerate the instances where this idea has guided their approach. It is enough to suggest that an enormous void—moreover, one installed within a historic structure, such as the 1887 Pension Building in Washington, D.C.—invites the project of a gossamer Tensegrity Bridge, or that the empty Gas Holders at King's Cross in London, where our architects propose apartment buildings within the cylindrical holds, converge on a "void within a void" for circulation and vegetation.

At Portsmouth, Wilkinson Eyre have planned the Mary Rose Museum, which will serve at once as a dry dock and tomb chamber for the hull of the unfortunate ship Henry VIII witnessed foundering in battle at sea. The building and the glass hull complementing the fragmentary ship that was

9

[3] Cited in: *Richard Deacon, Sculptures, 1987–1993.* Hanover: Kunstverein, 1993, p. 126

raised from the seabed will be turned into a time capsule. The strikingly timeless character of the capsule cradles and protects fragmentary relics of the past, not unlike the droplets of resin that trapped insects, pollen, and leaves and over time hardened into amber. A suspicion also hardens in our mind about the peculiar nature of industrial materials that promise to endure for very long spans of time, such as glass and stainless steel. Because they withstand time and its universally corrosive effects better than other materials, their cultural lot is to stem the force of historical time, its decay and degradation. Although these artificial materials are relative newcomers to architecture, when held to the scale of its evolution, they impose a chronology of their own. They tend toward norm and constancy, but when they change, they do so as a result of their production processes, rather than according to arbitrary formal decisions. Similarly, visitors to the Mary Rose Museum will be able to move across a kind of gangplank running through history as they pass between the conserved hull of the ship and the capsule holding its artifactual fragments.

The idea of a capsule—gargantuan by comparison to its cargo, or mere cocoon, as the case may be—makes its appearance as a hollow, a translucent shell, or a bridge-like structure vaulting a motorway, as the New Botanic Gardens in Newcastle are intended to do. Inquiring into the nature of these capsules, one may ask, as the English sculptor Richard Deacon asked himself in 1978–79, "what an enclosure is, and what an opening is. An enclosure," Deacon asserted, "is a clarification, actually; an opening is a possibility," just as "singing and listening are reciprocal activities."[3] With regard to his drawings Deacon concluded that they "seemed to show that what was enclosed had a relationship to the contour. This functioned like a skin over the interior, and the interior remained a hollow resonant space." It is precisely the

10

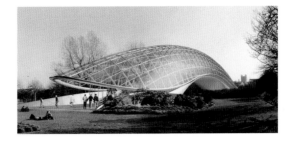

mutually defining rapport of hollow and contour that also imparts a specific "resonance" to Wilkinson Eyre's shells. Deacon detected that only in such a resonant hollow do "appearance, community, building, speaking, listening, production and manufacture all seem to be involved," as indeed they need to be in our architects' capsules. The intent to hold and conserve is of a piece with the notion of the capsule, which variously opens up to its site or beyond. It can take the shape of a half-buried, tent-like structure, as it does for the Alpine House at Kew Gardens, or of huge clam-shaped halls, as on the King's Waterfront in Liverpool.

The Albert Dock forms massive piles of unfaced brick which will find their counterpart in two silvery shells whose flowing lines and slightly asymmetrical halves will appear to breathe in the light and shade between the River Mersey and the usually luminous sky. Much hangs in the balance for a project that will provide a wide range of facilities, beginning with public transportation and parking, centering on arena, conference and exhibition facilities along the riverfront, and ending with amenities of site and residence, all expected to give new "resonance" to the town.

King's Waterfront will have to exert all the powers architecture can muster in order to breathe life into the site and bring energy to the city beyond the fanfare of its inauguration on the occasion of Liverpool's turn among the European Capitals of Culture in 2008. The project gives every promise of success. Similar initiatives too often hang on the hopes we hold out for technological solutions to problems that have defeated other efforts. We are inclined to defer to the imperatives raised by conditions of our own making rather than rethink them, and we gladly defer changing them when technological magic promises to turn things around. What Wilkinson Eyre are doing for the Mersey riverfront finds an impressive prelude in the nearby

Paradise Street Interchange—a tram and bus terminal, and a nearby car park whose ramps climb free of the structure's reticulate, ascending the length of six bays in order to reach the next higher floor. As the car park is ten bays in length and holds six storeys of parking, the lowest ramp sheers off the middle, and the others each hark back a bay, so that the lowest and the highest extend to opposite corners of the building. While it all seems eminently simple, not to mention compelling in its logic, there is no other car park quite like it anywhere else.

Here and elsewhere, Wilkinson Eyre develop their ideas from the conditions of site and purpose, but without the high rhetoric of programme-induced design. True, Wilkinson Eyre recognise what may be inalterable in a given project as well as that which is amenable to modifications, as only architects are able to conceptualise them. Bowing neither to functionalist dictates (even where they have resurfaced in more fashionable guise) nor to typological schemes of old, Wilkinson Eyre seek the figures that can hold the inevitable bundle of contradictory demands and still emerge as ideas. Where issues of engineering predominate, such figures may seem intrinsic to the task, as in the design of bridges, or they may assume an unpredictable character as they do with high-rise buildings. A caveat is in order, though, for neither our architects' bridges, like the pedestrian link between buildings used by the Royal Ballet School in London, nor their more conventional projects, such as schools, reside comfortably within the bounds of traditional categories.

Thinking of the gap between the mid-19th century and our current conditions suggests that one can cast a glance back across the long history of such ideas and at the same time gauge their significance for the future of our culture. Engineering must of course be recognised as something more than the underbelly of architecture or its repressed alter ego.

13

[4] Sigfried Giedion, *Bauen in Frankreich, Bauen in Eisen, Bauen in Eisenbeton.* Leipzig: Klinkhardt & Biermann, 1928. In recognition of the formative importance of Giedion's book, I decided to include it in the series *Texts & Documents,* which I initiated at the Getty Research Institute in 1986, and in which the English edition of the book, ed. by Sokratis Georgiadis and transl. by J. Duncan Berry, appeared in 1995 as the eighth in a series now grown to over twenty volumes. The series *Texts & Documents* was inaugurated by the English translation of Otto Wagner's *Modern Architecture,* ed. by Harry Francis Mallgrave.

[5] Gottfried Semper, *Wissenschaft, Industrie und Kunst: Vorschläge zur Anregung nationalen Kunstgefühles bei dem Schlusse der Londoner Industrie-Ausstellung,* London, den 11. Oktober 1851. Braunschweig: Vieweg, 1852

It was Sigfried Giedion who traced an interesting peripeteia of building technology in *Building in France, Building in Iron, Building in Ferro-Concrete* of 1928.[4] As we now know, the book "electrified"—to use his own words—Walter Benjamin, precisely because he, too, had begun to investigate the "unconscious" of historical transformations as it manifested itself (above ground and in the air) in glass and steel, whilst running deep underground and unwittingly undermining its foundations. Although old Gottfried Semper had considered the Crystal Palace "a glass-covered vacuum"[5] and never overcame his displeasure with the extremely attenuated shape of structural members in iron, his own evolutionary thinking traced so many significant steps in the past transformation of architecture that he might as well have dotted in the lines connecting that past to the present. For his part, Giedion did, recognising the all-important role of construction. And not just its exacting and pragmatic side: he intuited in "construction" more than "mere ratio."[6] Choosing the Eiffel Tower as an example in which engineering and "the basic aesthetic experience of today"[7] coincide, Giedion recognised the transformations that were to launch a virtually new architecture toward the end of the 19th century. Due to the fact that "the air drawn into the interior of the piers [of the Eiffel Tower] now becomes, in an unprecedented way, a formative material,"[8] construction addressed its hollows as earnestly as it did its solids across the millennia.

The Eiffel Tower was as impressive a feat of engineering and assembly as the Crystal Palace had been for the precedent-setting World's Fair of 1851. In London and Paris, the defenders of architecture as it was practiced lambasted Eiffel as a traitor to taste and culture. Serene and measured in his response, he defended himself brilliantly in the newspaper *Le Temps* on February 14, 1887, as construction of the Tower got underway. "Is it not true," he asked, "that

14

Detail of piers and long view, Eiffel Tower, Paris 1900.

[6] Giedion, *Building in France. Building in Iron, Building in Ferro-Concrete.* Santa Monica, CA: Getty Center, 1995, p.87. One might add that Henry-Russel Hitchcock, in a book appearing on the heels of Giedions's *Bauen in Frankreich,* [Henry-Russel Hitchcock, *Modern Architecture. Romanticism and Reintegration.* New York: Payson & Clarke, 1929, pp.40–51] devoted a rather unenthusiastic chapter to "Engineering and Building," though he did recognise, however reluctantly, the crucial role of construction in the emergence of the new architecture.

[7] Ibid., p.91

[8] Ibid., p.143

[9] Otto Wagner, *Modern Architecture,* ed. by Harry Francis Mallgrave. *Texts & Documents.* Santa Monica, CA: Getty Center for the History of Art and the Humanities, 1988, p.115

the very conditions which give strength also conform to the hidden rules of harmony? ... To what phenomenon did I have to give primary concern in designing the Tower? It was wind resistance. Well then, I hold that the curvature of the monument's four outer edges, which is as mathematical calculation dictated it should be, ... will give an impression of strength and beauty, for it will reveal to the eyes of the observer the boldness of the design as a whole. Likewise, the many empty spaces built into the very elements of construction will clearly display the constant concern not to submit any unnecessary surfaces to the violent action of hurricanes. For my part," Eiffel declared, "the Tower will possess its own beauty. Are we to believe that because one is an engineer, one is not preoccupied with beauty in one's constructions, or that one does not seek to create elegance as well as solidity and durability?"

Eiffel both adopts and subverts the old Vitruvian triad of *firmitas, utilitas, venustas*—solidity, utility, beauty—reclaiming the grounds of his critics for himself. Whilst suggesting that the Tower is both solid and durable, Eiffel slips in the word "elegance" to characterise its particular kind of "beauty." This may have been a concession to French taste, which expects beauty to convey itself through social grace rather than remain mysterious and aloof. Eiffel's talk of "elegance" also implies cunning, a shrewdness in overcoming physical and material limits. Craftiness and subtlety, too, resonate in the use of the term "elegance." We continue to grapple with the word today, for what is "elegant" neither claims to be "true," nor admits to be "false," but rather veers toward the "chic" and "graceful." But "elegance" also appeals to intelligence, and in this regard Eiffel shares a transcendent ideal with the Viennese architect Otto Wagner, who claimed, just a few years later, "that a country's art is the measure not only of its well-being, but also first and foremost of its *intelligence*."[9]

15

[10] Ibid., p. 92
[11] Ibid., p. 93
[12] Ibid., p. 98/99
[13] Ibid., p. 99
[14] Ibid., p. 2 of Introduction
[15] Ibid., p. 60
[16] See *The Work of Pier Luigi Nervi*, introduction by Ernesto N. Rogers. New York: Praeger, 1957. Nervi first built two airplane hangars in Orvieto in 1936 whose ribs were cast in place, but the hangars at Orbetello were assembled from pre-fabricated concrete segments, welded together in situ, and covered by concrete tiles. All of these hangars were dynamited during the retreat of the German army from Italy.

Eiffel argued that the shapes in his work of engineering obey the laws of physics, that of necessity they had to be the way they are. That argument soon resonated with Otto Wagner's argument that *artis sola domina necessitas*, that art is only ruled by necessity. Less than a decade younger than Eiffel, Wagner soon faced dilemmas in Vienna that paralleled Eiffel's in Paris, being obliged to explain his way of approaching major civic projects and public buildings. In his programmatic book *Modern Architecture* of 1896, Wagner picked up the major strands of discourse linking the historic origins of building to its technologically sophisticated descendents: "Every architectural form has arisen in construction and has successfully become an art-form."[10] By vesting such defining power in "construction," Wagner sought to bridge a gap that was widening during his lifetime, as engineers made extraordinary strides while many architects restricted themselves to a repertoire of historic forms. Wagner argued that "new purposes must give birth to new methods of construction, and by this reasoning also to new forms."[11] Forms were thus to be derived from the new, even when it was still unknown, rather than held over from the past. Where Wagner strained the conventional performance of materials, employing steel framing and letting it show, cladding façades with thin slabs, using aluminium and lattice-like cornices, he wished to demonstrate that "well-conceived construction not only is the prerequisite of every architectural work, but also, and this cannot be repeated often enough, provides the modern creative architect with a number of positive ideas for creating new forms."[12] Wagner went so far as to base his notion of the modern architect on "knowledge and experience of construction,"[13] an idea of his that was not lost on Mies van der Rohe and other architects growing up while Wagner held sway in Vienna.

16

Wagner, Post Office Savings Bank, Vienna (left). Wagner, Karlsplatz Station, Vienna (right).

[17] The "decorative engineering" has to come to haunt the work of Renzo Piano, for example. See Pier Luigi Nervi, *Aesthetics and Technology in Building,* transl. by Robert Einaudi. Cambridge, MA: Harvard University Press, 1965. In his Eliot Norton lectures, Nervi explained the structural principles and differences between the two types of hangars. He also affirmed his conviction that "as the design proceeded and became clearer, I saw again how a purely technical process also brought aesthetic results and suggested promising architectural directions" (p. 99).

Critics of Wagner took aim at what they considered to be his pragmatic (some might say cynical) view of modern urban life and his connection with French engineering (a mixture apparently considered explosive), when they called him "a show-off addicted to originality, a worshipper of an affected, brutal, Gallic architectural materialism."[14] What got him into trouble was precisely the "elegance" of an Eiffel that was now decried as "affected" and "Gallic." That a major shift had occurred we gather from Wagner's assertion that "we must become fully aware that the sole departure point for our artistic work can only be modern life."[15] This kind of realism embraced the demographic conditions of the city, its planned expansion, the requirements of modern transportation, the incongruities of scale and class, the tenor of a different life. Instead of betting single-mindedly on one or another solution as a panacea against all ills, Wagner calmly accepted terms that seemed inalterable and proceeded with assurance.

Whereby we return to Wilkinson Eyre, whose works at once belong to and transcend their traditional categorisation. In the mid-1990s, they designed a huge train shed, the Stratford Market Depot near the terminus of the newly opened Jubilee Line of the London underground. With a nod of recognition to Nervi, whose airplane hangar at Orbetello had been constructed with cross-braced concrete arches,[16] Wilkinson Eyre employed a system of tubular trusses that unload their weight on branching columns at the periphery of the hangar. More than an example of productive imitation, this is an ingenious demonstration of transformative thinking. Inspired perhaps by the parallelogram of the roof with respect to the parallel tracks, the diagonally shifted sides (acknowledged in the directional skylights) may have prompted a system of interlocking trusses.[17]

The shed shares nothing with the recent vogue for "decorative engineering," which has come to haunt the

17

Nervi, Aircraft Hangar, Orbetello (above). Internal structure, Stratford Market Depot, London (opposite). Model detail, Guangzhou West Tower, Guangzhou (opposite top).

[18] The recently completed Paul Klee Foundation at Bern betrays the familiar dilemma that arises when a beautiful and lithe idea is realised in rather crudely engineered fashion. The project promised a hovering triple wave, rising with the elegance of a manta's body from the hilly ground of its surroundings, but the actual building plays up the armature of its curving beams, at once skeletal—hence of a dead ray rather than a life one in motion—and overtly technicistic. Where the bending ribs hit the ground and partly disappear in the gravel, the contrast between real nature (even real dirt) and the organic shape of the building turns problematic.

work of Renzo Piano,[18] for example, and which may have had much to do with the international success of so-called English High Tech architecture since the 1970s. Where technology comes to the fore in the work of Wilkinson Eyre, it is indeed purposeful and pretty "high" for that matter. For their project of two towers in a recent extension of Guangzhou, China, toward the Pearl River, they fashion elegantly tapering buildings that exceed the height of the Eiffel tower by a third. The architects smooth a triangular shaft down to the perfection of a late-neolithic scraper —then use it against the sky rather than matter. Braced by a triangular lattice (each triangle extending through six storeys) which registers on the façades as an internal structure without compromising the pristine sheath of the tower, the project solicits comparison with recent towers in London and Barcelona. Whilst rejecting the iconic closure of Foster's Swiss Re or the pixelated costume of Nouvel's, Wilkinson Eyre's Guangzhou tower would fall nothing short of the ambition to create a perfect shape, and at the same time owe nothing in terms of optical effect, insofar as its surface like polished stone implies its sheer material identity.

The expanse of today's urbanised lands has given bridge construction a new lease on life. Well beyond their undeniable utility, bridges still carry associations strong enough to kindle the collective imagination. Heated political controversies routinely surround their proposal and construction, as in the case of the bridge over the Strait of Messina, and competition over the length and height of their spans never fails to flare up around them. Bridges always pose the problem of construction and assembly under tricky topographical conditions that call for such structures in the first place. Not the least part of the builder's ingenuity goes into anticipating an economical way of transporting and assembling the parts that need to be joined on site.

18

What the Stratford Market Depot did for Wilkinson Eyre's emergence as a firm with the capacity to handle projects calling for complex engineering, the Gateshead Millenium Bridge accomplished in the domain of bridge construction. Wilkinson Eyre's ability to find a perfect fit between the specific purpose and site of a bridge has been put to the test in three major crossings so far: the Poole Harbour Second Crossing, the Nescio Bridge in Amsterdam, and the Gateshead Millennium Bridge. Each is based on a different principle, responds specifically to the requirements of the site, and invokes an image of its performance. By linking the nature of the architectural image to the type of crossing the bridge needs to make, I mean to suggest that although the image necessarily preceded the bridge, Wilkinson Eyre succeeded each time in collapsing bridge and image into a metaphor of the particular nature of a specific crossing. Moreover, each of these three bridges transforms its location into a site of ingenuity, rendering memorable what would be, without its presence, a fairly nondescript stretch of water.

The suburban link with a landfill island north of Amsterdam snakes across the canal in a side-winding motion that plays down its suspension from two pylons to the point of insignificance. Would it be an exaggeration to speak of a flying snake? The Poole Harbour Crossing, on the other hand, folds down into a causeway, when it doesn't sheer open, unlocking its sail-shaped segments as it lifts them in homage to the yachts cruising through the strait. Finally, the architects themselves have likened the rotational movement of the Gateshead Millennium Bridge to a slowly opening eyelid. Surely, the twisting accordion of the Royal Ballet bridge in London, linking two buildings across Floral Street in Covent Garden, encourages one to think in ways that defy both conventional associations with passerelles and a tendency to limit engineering to pedestrian roles.

21

[19] Kurt W. Forster, "A Word into the Ear of the Giant," in: *Parkett*, 69 (2003), p. 104. One of the early signs of activity in the area was set in 1990, when Richard Deacon installed his coloured steel piece *Once upon a Time* on the former Redheugh Bridge; see Richard Deacon, *Sculptures*, 1987–1993. Hanover: Kunstverein, 1993, p. 171

[20] See the monographic issue of *Architectural Design* on "Folding in Architecture," ed. by Greg Lynn; with a new introduction by Greg Lynn and Mario Carpo. Chichester, UK/Hoboken, NJ: Wiley-Academy, 2004

Each bridge not only answers its unique requirements but also conjures an *image* fashioned from its structural or functional essence. Each bends type to its own purpose, while extending the reach of its model. No Calatrava could have made so lean a shape and so airy a pair of arches as those at Gateshead, distinct in their purpose yet tightly locked into affinity. Wilkinson Eyre do not yield to the temptation of making the peacock spread its fanned tail, but simply allow the component parts of the bridge—two parabolic curves—to perform. As an intimation, the moving "eyelids" match the delicacy of the double curvature with its graceful balance, as well as its cyclical movement day and night. Gateshead is indeed looking up, after a series of catalytic attempts have led to complete renovation of the areas on both embankments. Lord Foster's Concert Hall now redraws the profile of the hillside using the current technology of envelopes to house two conventionally conceived halls under a undulating enclosure, while the nearby Baltic Mills are the periodic venue of such installations as Anish Kapoor's *Taratantara*.[19]

If I conclude with a project that will not see the light of day, that is only because it represents yet another facet of Wilkinson Eyre's approach. The King Alfred Development intends to install a new landmark on the Brighton seafront, mixing (as has become obligatory) public and private facilities, open zones and restricted uses. What seaside piers may have accomplished in the past, allowing visitors to detach themselves from the land and yet enjoy a safe platform on which (as James Ivory's film *The Remains of the Day* so poignantly narrated) harmless amusements and cathartic experiences could be had for the asking, today's projects must contend with more public and yet more introverted flights of fancy. The convoluted nature of our experiences and the constant reversal of inside and outside

22

Anish Kapoor, Taratantara *1999
(left). Model, King Alfred
Development, Hove (right).*

pervade Wilkinson Eyre's proposal, based as it is on a
continuous ribbon folding back and forth whilst zigzaging
landward and seaward.

Folding was, of course, a familiar strategy for generating
design in the later 1980s and early 1990s,[20] widely employed
and rather quickly abandoned, but what Wilkinson Eyre
were after with their project at Brighton is closely bound
up with the differentiation of volumes as a way of making
their differences register and resonate within one another.
They built a model which, when its interiors are lit, conveys
the torsion affecting each block and the elastic potential
of their interaction. It is fair to say that the architects were
channeling all the weight of complex problems through
a kind of motion-simulator, as if to test their idea to see
if it would fly. What was still a regularly scaled series of
closely ranged blocks for the National Waterfront Museum
in Swansea would have turned at Brighton into exfoliated
volumes seesawing against one another. Their relationship
would have changed in the blink of a visitor's eye, whilst
keeping a grip on the intricacies of our highly organised
lives. Not an unfair way of looking at the work of our
architects, and certainly an accurate picture of their abilities.

The Magic Carpet
by Peter Davey

One of the most powerful designs to have emerged from the
Wilkinson Eyre practice is a bridge in North-West Greece.
The deck, carried simply on a slender curve of high tensile
steel cables, conveys the road from cliff face to cliff face of
the narrow cleft carved into the Pindos Mountains by the
river Metsovitikos. On each side, the road is tunnelled into
the rock and the cables are fixed directly to anchorages on
the rock faces, so no supporting towers are needed. Working
with Arup, the architects reduced the suspension bridge to
its simplest possible form, a spare and elegant horizontal
plane between the chasm walls—the archetypal magic
carpet, flying in light and air between caverns in the cliffs.

Sadly, the project will not be built because the client
abandoned the scheme, yet the design demonstrates many
of the architects' most characteristic and powerful qualities.
It shows determination to push to the edge of known
possibilities and to investigate and use creative imagination
and the potential of modern technologies, to explore and
extend boundaries of the possible. At the same time, it is a
link—a literal one between the two sides of the valley, but
simultaneously it connects the life of our times to immemorial
geological form, the present to history, and specificity of
place to the global generality of the technological culture
that makes today's world work.

All good architecture has many dimensions, and Wilkinson
Eyre's work can be explored from numerous points of view.
One of its most significant characteristics is its continual
inventiveness. The practice has no house style (too often a
sign of architects who have run out of ideas or who are stuck
in a groove). Nor has it restricted itself to a set of readily
identifiable formal tropes (usually the sign of architects who
are more interested in themselves than anything else).
Unless informed in advance, you surely could not tell that,
for instance, the Magna project in Rotherham, which

Contextual and deck views,
Metsovitikos Bridge, Greece.

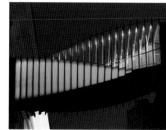

reinvents a huge superannuated industrial building, and the Royal Ballet School's Bridge of Aspiration twisting high above London's Covent Garden were designed by the same firm—nor that the Kew Alpine House and the Swansea Waterfront Museum emerged from the same stable.

But Wilkinson Eyre do have some predilections. For instance, their choices of materials and technologies tend to be based on High Tech tradition, and their approach often involves innovatory applications of engineering and other disciplines. Though neither Chris Wilkinson nor Jim Eyre is an engineer, they have shown that they can work with a range of technical consultants to generate coherent works of great integrity. As Jim Eyre says, "while a working understanding of the capabilities of other disciplines, trades and specialisms has always been in the architect's remit, now science . . . is so complex that every area requires specialism, but nevertheless, while one can no longer meaningfully complete a complex design alone . . . the spatial, structural, formal and 'light and colour' possibilities unleashed mean that distinct boundaries between disciplines are more ambiguous." Indeed, the firm is committed to extending and blurring boundaries between traditional disciplines.

As much contemporary architecture shows, it takes a lot of skill to manage a process of design that must necessarily involve many participants: too often, the result is an incoherent mess or an over-rigid attempt by the architect to impose order at any cost. But the way in which Wilkinson Eyre work with their consultants is similar to the creative process of design evolution in their own office. Chris Wilkinson and Jim Eyre lead small teams of architects on different projects. Directors suggest but do not dictate, and the team collaborates to achieve what Wilkinson calls a "beautiful solution." Well run, the process is clearly

26

exhilarating, causing director Paul Baker to enthuse about "the joy of collaborative thought" in a small design team.

For Wilkinson Eyre, one of the keys to creating a beautiful solution is specificity. Analysis of each project begins by exploring context and programme without preconceptions. Context in this sense does not simply mean the physical nature of the site and its environs (its topography, vegetation, micro climate, visual characteristics and so on) but its history, and social and cultural implications—in short, everything that makes the site a particular place. Onto this empirical exploration, the pragmatic requirements of the brief are layered and woven during the design process until a solution begins to emerge.

A striking instance of this layering of programme to site is the genesis of the Swansea National Waterfront Museum (p. 76). There remaining fragments of railway track that served the port in its industrial heyday are not only preserved but help to generate the planning geometry of the new complex. Another notable example of the approach is the daring design for the exhibition hall at Crystal Palace (p. 68), in which the new glass-clad volume hovers precisely over the axis and foundations of the transverse aisle of the great Victorian building. Its height is the same as the aisle, so from central London, it will evoke Paxton's presence without in the least resorting to pastiche. The Magna project in Rotherham (p. 48) is specifically intended to evoke the past, and it does this by imaginatively repairing the vast shed—but being careful to leave scars and perforations as reminders of the Promethean forces that were contained in it. Earth, air, fire and water (all the Aristotelian elements involved in steel making) are evoked in individual pavilions that provide zones of clarity, light and heat within the nebulous dark area—destinations on a journey through time and space in which all the human senses, even scent, are dramatically involved.

27

As part of their concern with exploring particularity of place and programme, the notion of destination is important to Wilkinson Eyre. Some of their buildings are real destinations, like the Stratford station (completed 1999). It links the underground, overground and Docklands Light Rail systems with ingenious geometry and creates a grand hall that made a real contribution to its part of London and initiated a process of regeneration in a previously much ignored and run-down part of the city. But Wilkinson Eyre's destinations are not necessarily components of transport systems. A more recent instance of destination-making is the Guangzhou tower (p. 160), a landmark designed to put the city on the world's mental map, to help give it identity and to be a symbol of its citizens' aspirations. In a similar way, the urban interventions at Gateshead, Swansea, Liverpool, IJburg and Crystal Palace are all intended to attract attention to their cities or districts, and to help revitalise them by drawing on the past to regenerate the present.

Spectacle is one of the devices used to make the buildings memorable and therefore attractive as centres of regeneration. Spectacle is characteristic of much contemporary architecture, but Wilkinson Eyre's exploration of spectacle is completely different from that of many architects, who want to impose their brand (in both senses of the word) on cities as different as Seattle and Singapore, Berlin and Beijing. The Gateshead Millennium Bridge (p. 36) is a dramatic example of Wilkinson Eyre's approach to spectacle: a quite remarkable reworking of an ancient type, the river crossing that can be adjusted to allow precedence either to waterborne or to land-based traffic. But there has never been a bridge like this one. When its two delicate arcs rotate upwards to herald the passage of a ship, they pay reverence to the curve of the Tyne Bridge further upstream. Yet it is the moving, dynamic bridge that attracts spectators,

29

and it has already replaced the older structure as the icon of the area, a recognition to be reinforced when it appears on English pound coins. It has the same sort of iconic power as London's Tower Bridge, but it is much more delicate and integrated than the Victorian conjunction of brute engineering and the neo-gothic.

Other bridges explore different kinds of spectacle. Hovering midway between sculpture and engineering, the bridge proposed for the Pension Building in Washington will change continuously as its integral lighting alters in response to the stresses imposed by people walking across it. It will undoubtedly become one of the sights of the U.S. capital. One of the practice's favourite tactics is to celebrate the act of progression, literally raising the spirits, by moving dramatically into light and air from dark and undistinguished approaches: what might be called the Metsovitikos gambit. At the smallest scale, this is the scenario used in the Royal Ballet School's "Bridge of Aspiration" (p. 102) where from both sides, after muddling through boring and totally unmemorable passages, you suddenly come to the elation of the astonishing, dancing space high up above the street. On a much larger scale, the same is true of the Gatwick airbridge (p. 152), where, after plodding along what seem to be hundreds of metres of anonymous airport corridors, you are suddenly, surprisingly, in daylight, walking over the huge aeroplanes in which you are going to take off. Magna, by the way, is in a sense a reversal of these tactics; there, the bridges are routes through mysterious darkness between the light and drama of the pavilions.

For all of Wilkinson Eyre's fascination with spectacle, their work is never driven by formal considerations alone, unlike that of the self-indulgent gestural architects, whose caperings have been so extensively illustrated in the last couple of decades. Wilkinson Eyre's formal moves are always based on

30

Tensegrity Bridge, Washington DC (opposite). Elevation and interior, Stratford Regional Station, London (above).

function or empathy—usually a combination of both. Thus, no matter how huge one of their landmark buildings may be, it always retains human scale near the ground. The buildings are welcoming and celebrate the magic threshold moment of movement from outside to inside.

To achieve this command of form, it is necessary to have a thorough command of geometry, and the work has demonstrated some quite remarkable geometrical tours de force—the most obviously dramatic of which is the Ballet School's bridge, a solution that creatively reconciles the different alignments and heights of its approaches with astonishing geometrical originality and skill. A thorough understanding of the craft and process of building is as important as geometry. British architects of the last half century have been blessed with a couple of generations of innovative, imaginative and helpful engineers who initially astounded the world with radical structures, but who in recent years have extended their range to environmental and other aspects of the design process. Like some of the exponents of British High Tech, Wilkinson Eyre have worked fruitfully with engineering consultants, but without (unlike some of the more extreme High Tech exponents) being overwhelmed by them, or becoming obsessed by the forms of late 20th century technology. Technology is never the master; it is always made subservient to human values.

Virtually all the best architects in the world are responding to the planet's environmental crisis. Wilkinson Eyre's initial involvement with structural issues has broadened into inventively exploring environmental elements of design. For instance, at Stratford, the curving roof is not just a welcoming and comforting shape but a key element in the solar-assisted ventilation, for as the roof is heated by the sun it acts as a thermal chimney, conducting air from the concourse up to be discharged at the eaves. One of the most recent results of this

31

concern with sustainability is the remarkably ingenious Alpine House at Kew Gardens (p. 58). Alpines need a cool climate with a gentle constant flow of air, yet they also have to thrive on as much daylight and sunshine as possible. The requirements almost seem mutually contradictory and are certainly difficult to achieve in a glass house a few metres above sea level. But Wilkinson Eyre, working with environmental engineers Atelier Ten, produced a low-energy building by using the cooling principle employed by termites in their mounds, where air is drawn in at low level and cooled in underground chambers. At Kew the cooled air flows over the plants before rising upwards by convection to be expelled at the apex. Elegant fan-like devices rise automatically to shade the plants when the sun's heat threatens to become too intense. Plenty of people are experimenting with low-energy structures, but few have produced anything so ingenious and original.

Kew is a small, dramatic and intense example of sustainability, but the principles are being applied to even the largest projects in many different ways. For instance, the double skin walls proposed for the Guangzhou towers contain a louvre system that will greatly reduce solar heat gain. The glass shell of the Crystal Palace gazebo gallery encapsulates photovoltaic cells that provide the energy to drive the climate control systems of the space. Perhaps the most extensive use of such thinking is in the exemplar schools (p. 118) where, among other measures, there will be no artificial cooling (save in IT areas); most ventilation will be by convection and heating fuel will be locally grown biomass.

The schools programme, and its first built project, the John Madejski Academy, are further examples of Wilkinson Eyre's continuing concern for regeneration and urban form. Stratford was one of the first major Wilkinson Eyre urban interventions intended to renew and strengthen decayed and

33

fringe urban areas. Others include of course, the Gateshead and the IJburg bridges, Magna, Swansea and the Brighton Marina project. The Liverpool King's Waterfront (p. 90) is by far their largest regeneration-related project so far. Like the Swansea National Waterfront Museum, it is intended to bring lively new uses to its area, and like the Welsh project, it engages physically with the city at many levels. For example, from the Mersey, it is intended to complement the dramatic cityscape by defining an axis between the waterfront and the two cathedrals on their ridge. At closer range, the new urban space created within the complex is inflected towards the city centre so that it can become an organic extension of the traditional fabric, a physical link which is expected to induce social ones: in the architects' terms, the new development will become a destination within the city.

Destinations deserve to be celebrated by landmarks, and Wilkinson Eyre are not afraid of creating them—though, unlike many well-known contemporary architects, they do not so for self-aggrandisation or showing off. One of the most thought-provoking recent landmark projects is the re-use and relocation of the gas holders at King's Cross (p.126) as housing to act as a reminder of the history of the site and to signal the much overdue radical redevelopment of the largest derelict site in central London as a series of new urban spaces. The tower at Brighton Marina (p. 146) serves the same purpose, as a signal to both land and sea, a marker of the new destination, but its colour (and to some extent form) draw on the white architecture of the resort's seafront and the curves of sails in the wind.

In some ways, Wilkinson Eyre are part of the British picturesque tradition, with its love of progression along routes that join events (both expected and unexpected) in a pictorial narrative. But, unlike the great picturesque designers of

34

King's Waterfront, Liverpool (opposite top). Façade study, King's Cross Gas Holders, London (opposite bottom). Air pavilion, Magna, Rotherham (left). Model, Mary Rose Museum, Portsmouth (right).

the 18th century such as William Kent or Lancelot Brown, Wilkinson Eyre rarely try to identify the nature of the events they create: meaning is for users and spectators to provide. Exceptions are of course, Magna and the Mary Rose, where the architects and exhibition designers explicitly wish to evoke Aristotle's elements and to portray life in the Tudor navy.

Picturesque Wilkinson Eyre's work may be, but it is always imbued with a thoroughly Puginian respect for truth, both to materials and to function. Like Pugin, they believe that architecture is not an autonomous art intended for the sole gratification of its practitioners and their clients, but a discipline that should serve everyone. Wilkinson Eyre's work is as much concerned with its human implications as its artistic ones, but the architects are not afraid of asserting their artistic nature. They think of their designs as fusions of art and science, but the art component is just as important as the technological one.

By mentioning some of Wilkinson Eyre's relationships to British traditions like the picturesque, Puginism and High Tech, I do not wish to imply that they are in the least provincial. As the projects shown here demonstrate, their approaches of searching out the specificity of programme and place, of relating contemporary life to history and context, and of reconciling art and technology, work wherever they are applied. The practice continues to be remarkably imaginative and innovative, so this book is an interim statement on a continuously evolving creative process.

Gateshead Millennium Bridge Gateshead, UK, 2001

Architecture has been called on to play a remarkably important part in the regeneration of the cities of the Industrial Revolution in the north of England. When traditional sources of wealth dried up, Gateshead tried more than most to turn its economy round from being based on industry to one that is hoped to be driven by services, shopping and culture. Seen from Newcastle on the north bank of the River Tyne, the city's efforts are immediately apparent. The old Baltic Flour Mills have been transformed into the Baltic Centre—the largest and perhaps the most lively centre for contemporary arts in the region. Close to the Baltic's massive concrete early 20th century industrial forms is the Millennium Bridge, a pedestrian and cycleway which links the two cities across the Tyne.

In planning terms, it was conceived to be a catalyst for the regeneration of the decayed east Gateshead waterfront and to reinforce the creation of the city's new cultural quarter. In urban terms, it was required to be an attraction in itself, drawing people to the area by its presence. In functional terms, the bridge had to allow river traffic to be unimpeded, while being only some 5m over high water to allow convenient low-level connections for pedestrians and cyclists to the quays on both banks. A moving bridge was the obvious solution, offering the possibility of creating a memorable spectacle to celebrate linking the two cities and their regeneration.

37

Such devices have a distinguished history. Some say that the Romans had them (it would be surprising if they didn't), but they really became possible on a large scale in the 19th century, when steam power made possible such wonders as the twin bascules of London's Tower Bridge, the Runcorn Transporter Bridge (now sadly no more) and the Newcastle Swing Bridge which is only a little way up the Tyne from the Millennium Bridge. Here, the central section can swivel until it is parallel to the banks of the river, opening a channel for shipping on each side of the central island with its rotating engine.

Wilkinson Eyre built on this great tradition in their winning entry for the 1997 international competition, but their proposal was quite different from any moving bridge that had ever been made before. A parabolic arc of foot and cycleway deck is echoed by the curve of its supporting structure. The two are stiffened by their curved shape and are connected by 40mm stainless steel rods. Both curves have common springing points, and the two can be rotated together on top of new concrete islands (caissons) that bear onto the river bed. When they move, the curves balance each other, reducing loads on the eight electric motors that provide turning power. So when a boat wants to go under the bridge, the two curves are swivelled until, when seen end-on from the banks of the river, they form a great V with the almost invisible tension members horizontal. Seen from a boat coming up the middle of the river, the bridge becomes a huge ceremonial welcoming arch. From all angles, it catches the light with its two curves, one rounded and the other sharp against the sky.

Jim Eyre: The site owes its presence to the array of historic bridges in close proximity. The installation of the complete bridge, apparently hanging by a thread from the massive crane, alters the composition in a moment. Along with Armstrong's early swing bridge beyond, the new link completes a one-mile circular promenade at quayside level for the first time (main image).

The short but memorable journey up the Tyne from the Wallsend shipyards past the old cranes, seemingly defies the decline of an era of industrial might, evoking the new, forward-looking and optimistic spirit of the city (middle left).

The scale of the bridge can be seen in this section of the arch under construction (top). On opening day, 17 September 2001, the very first craft ceremoniously pass in line under the newcomer (bottom).

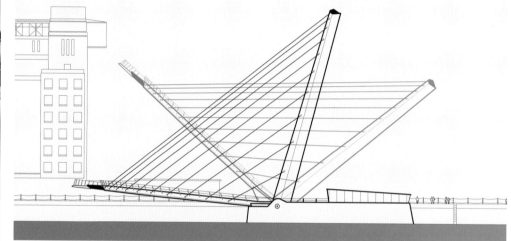

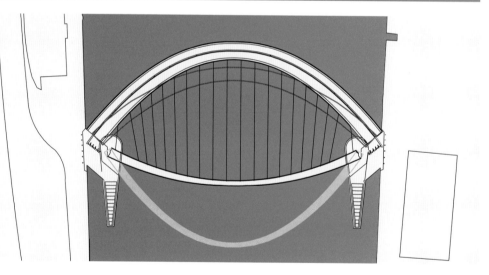

The whole dramatic process, much more spectacular than the movement of the swing bridge, takes four and a half minutes and is usually witnessed by an admiring crowd —the spectacular bridge really has become an attraction in its own right, as Gateshead Council hoped. And it fulfils another of the client's aspirations by not detracting from the picturesque Tyneside scene that continues to be dominated by the famous Tyne Bridge. Though the top of the Millennium Bridge's bearing arch is some 50m above the river, the 1920s road bridge (reputedly the ancestor of Sydney Harbour Bridge) still dominates the scene, the more so because the new arc resonates visually with the arch of the older crossing.

The Millennium Bridge (designed with engineers Gifford & Partners) spans 105m clear, and its length (because of the curve) is 126m. The caissons are clad in precast white concrete above the water line; on top of each caisson is a small glazed hall which can be used for exhibitions and offers new and powerful views of the river banks. The bridge itself is a finely-honed prefabricated structure which weighs some 850 tons; it was hoisted into place by the largest inshore floating crane in the world. Detailed design is as precise and thoughtful as that of the engineering. Two parallel decks form the bridge itself. The inner deck with its epoxy surface is formed on top of the specially fabricated main beam of the curving structure.

At each end the bridge rests on trunnion bearings which are expressed to reveal the ability for the structure to rotate, powered by hydraulic rams below (left).

The particular constraints of the physical brief (no structure on the quays, the need to avoid an overly steep gradient where the bridge to cross in a straight line and a requirement for a limited 25m height clearance) combine with the unwritten aspiration of the cultural-civic brief to lead to such a specific design (right).

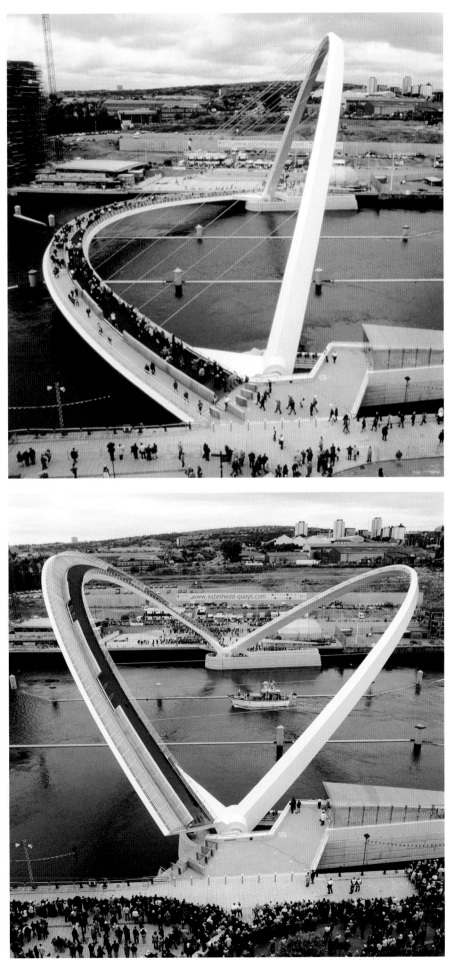

The structure acts as a performance piece as it effects its transformation from closed to open, and closed again. The intent is to provide a spectacle, but of few elements, each refined and appropriate to its engineering purpose (left).

Between just two arches separated by cables, a vast space is captured which must be circumnavigated by pedestrians and passed through by boats in turn (right).

Working with a structure already intended as an urban intervention or "event," itself seeking to re-energise and engender civic pride, Spencer Tunick's installation on 17 July 2005 spoke on many levels. Reasserting the crossing over of domains in art, architecture and engineering, perceived boundaries became blurred. Bridge metaphors for joining communities were heightened, while introducing tensions between innocence or vulnerability and hard steel, and the almost shocking notion of human commodity with the participants carried by the bridge as vessel (right).

The outer deck is for cyclists and has an aluminium grille surface intended to be safe and freely drained in all weathers; in some lights, when the bridge is rotated, the aluminium becomes a shining semi-transparent arc leaping between the two cities. To keep the two kinds of traffic physically separate but connected visually, the pedestrian deck is some 300mm higher than the cycling one, allowing a higher barrier on the lower side. A range of specially designed structures was developed for gates, balustrades and seats, which are provided every 30m along the bridge and form part of what the architects call the "hedges"—metre-high panels separating the decks. Such elements are made from specially patterned, perforated stainless steel, so during the day they seem reassuringly solid, but at night they glow with internal illumination, as part of the continuous and continuously variable lighting of the decks. Extraordinarily, detailed design helps keep the crossing clean, for anything loose dropped onto the decks rolls into special traps at each end of the bridge every time it is opened.

Unusually, both professions and public agree that the bridge is a masterpiece: a remarkable fusion of picturesque sensibility, engineering excellence, careful detailing and sheer invention. It really does seem to be putting Gateshead on the map as the Council that commissioned it intended. It won the Stirling Prize of the RIBA for the best building in the United Kingdom in 2002; it was on the first class postage stamps, and in 2007, it will be in everyone's pockets on the new pound coin.

Gateshead Metropolitan Borough Council (client); Bennett Associates; Gifford & Partners; Harbour & General Works; Speirs and Major Associates; Watson Steel

The rotated structure suggests motifs in specific views, here the symbol for infinity (bottom). Likened to an eye opening, one could also see the transparent mouth of a leviathan opening to swallow craft entering the city (main image).

46

Magna Rotherham, UK, 2001

The Templebrough steelworks at Rotherham was the largest foundry in Europe until it was closed in 1993. The city's economy was collapsing as traditional heavy industry was becoming uneconomic because of overseas competition from countries with cheaper labour. But the city council was not prepared to give up. It was determined to build a new, largely knowledge-based economy on the ruins of the old one. Nowhere was this more clear than at Templebrough, where casting may have ceased but the huge monumental building remained.

Instead of having it pulled down, the council appointed Wilkinson Eyre in 1998 to analyse how the great shed could be adapted to become a science adventure centre. With the aid of a Millennium Commission grant funded by the National Lottery, help from the European Union and from other sources, public and private existing buildings were reorganised, and new works installed to enable the centre to open in 2001.

The great legacy from the industrial past was a vast space of two 35m high bays of the foundry, 350m long. Externally, few changes have been made. Some ancillary buildings, principally the old scrap and concast (continuous casting) delivery bays on the north side have been stripped away to let the great mass speak. Here a new elevation is clad in profiled steel. Elsewhere the existing profiled skin has been repaired, and the whole has been painted black to emphasise the mass. In the car park, the uprights of the crane rail supports are retained as an almost filigree contrast to the huge black bulk. The structure of the old external crane rails and hoppers is retained for the same reason.

49

Nine-storey high transverse aisles form a grand entrance which is dominated by an original mass concrete concaster in much the way that huge statues of pharaohs dominated the entrance to Egyptian temples. Inside, the awesome volume is emphasised by leaving small holes caused by wear and tear in the profiled cladding, so on sunny days the space is pierced by thin sharp rays of light that gradually disappear into the darkness. Original devices used in the steel-making process are preserved as strange sculptures, and the shed's rusted steel structure is left untreated to show the wounds and scorchings caused by the terrifying Promethean processes the place was originally built to house.

Its present purpose is to explain the processes in terms of Aristotle's four elements: earth, air, fire and water, all of which are essential for steel production. Each element is demonstrated in a separate pavilion, designed in collaboration with Event Communications. The pavilions are oases of modern light, delicacy and colour amid the austere rusty darkness of late Industrial Revolutionary space. Air is represented by a large dirigible that seems to hover in the vast cavern, but is in fact hung by specially made aluminium extrusions from the existing steel structure that supported the gantry cranes. Its walls are made from a triple skin of translucent ETFE cushions kept in shape by air pressure; they are fixed to cigar-shaped steel beams that also carry the steel plate flooring. Air in many manifestations is examined from the creation of clouds to the force of a gale (there's a wind tunnel you can walk into); an (intentionally) wobbly suspension bridge leads to a showing of the Tacoma Narrows film to show the power of air at its most awesome.

Chris Wilkinson: On our first visit to the building it was still in its raw state, and we were struck by the vast scale and drama of the dark, vacant spaces. This huge piece of industrial archaeology possessed many of the qualities of a Gothic cathedral which we were determined to keep intact (top left and centre).

An early hand drawing shows the concept for four pavilions representing the Aristotelian elements of earth, fire, air and water (top right).

The flame-coloured fibreglass wall on the east elevation provides a red glow to the inside space during the day and on the outside at night. In this way it makes an apocryphal reference back to the immense heat and fire from the old steel furnaces that lit up the buildings in the past (main image).

50

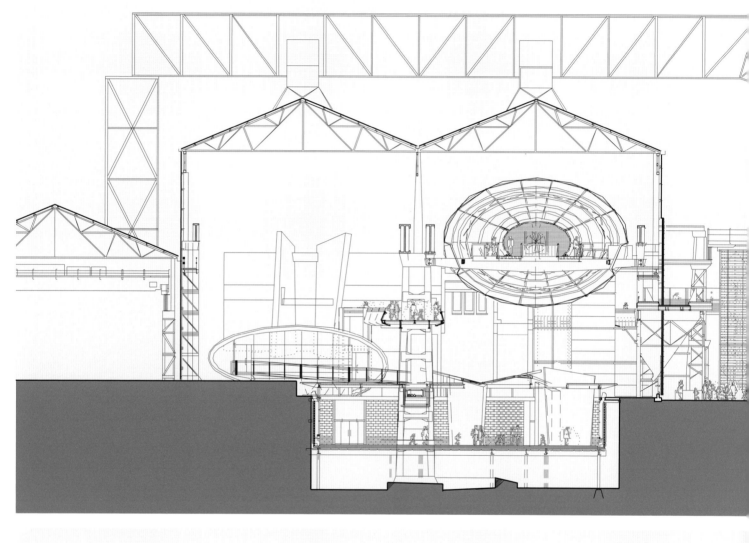

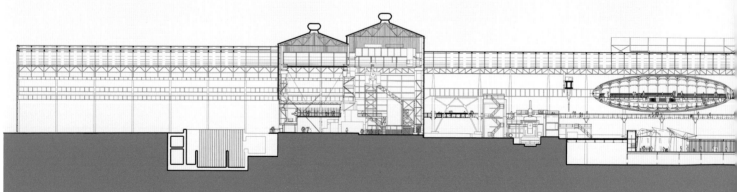

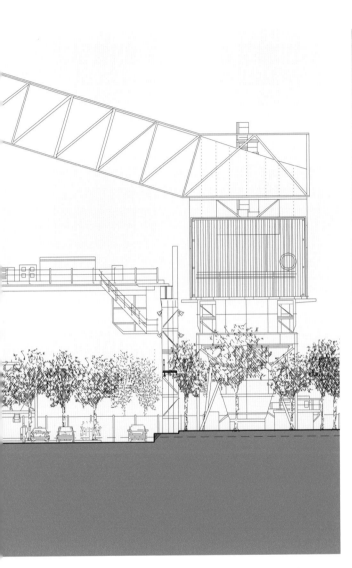

Drawings of the whole building emphasise the immense scale of the retained structure which acts as a container for the new pavilions (left).

During construction, the elliptical form of the water pavilion can be clearly seen, fabricated from a complex bending of tubular steelwork (top right).

The air pavilion is constructed out of inflated ETFE cushions connected by aluminium extrusions, and is held in place by tension wires attached to the main building structure. A steel compression ring at each end provides a former for setting out the structure (bottom right).

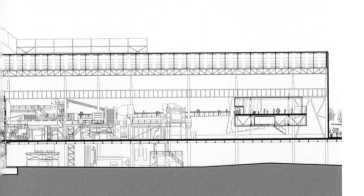

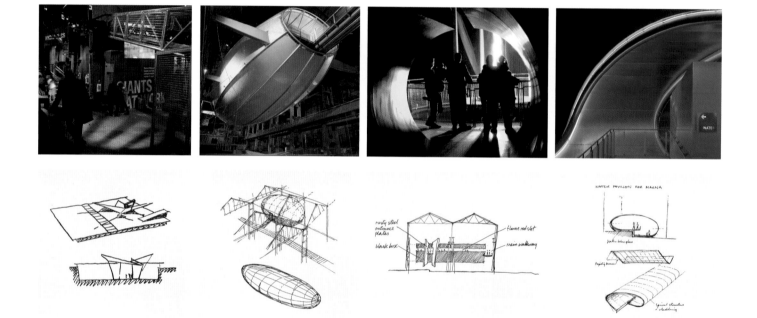

Early sketches explore the concepts for each pavilion and photographs show the finished results. In this building, the architecture expresses the themes of the exhibition in quite a literal and poetic way (opposite page).

Visitors explore the building on raised walkway bridges that link up the pavilions. In the centre of the main aisle, the air pavilion (left) is clearly visible to the right at high level, and the elliptical shape of the water pavilion can be seen below to the left of the walkway. The fire pavilion, located at the far end of the space, glows red through the entrance slot and provides a dramatic destination in its own right (bottom).

The fire pavilion, a charred black box—actually covered in a proprietary composite cladding, is dramatically suspended from the main structure with main support trusses spanning 41m across the two main aisles. Its exhibits are as inventive as those in the air pavilion, ranging from walls that respond to the heat of your body to frighteningly loud high voltage lightening discharges overhead.

The water pavilion is a stainless steel spiral ellipse structure 46m long in which children are encouraged to squirt and spill; it contains serious stuff, too, like an explanation of the water cycle and how water was (and is) used in the production of steel.

The earth pavilion is suspended 5m below ground level (the original factory floor) so that only the angled planes of its rusted steel roof are visible from above. Its exhibits range from explanations of how to blow up a quarry face to why the steel industry grew up in the area (largely because of ready availability of the three minerals needed for steel production: coal, iron ore and limestone).

The pavilions are linked to each other, and to the great and sometimes threatening devices that remain from the old processes, with new walkways that show off pavilions and the grand original works in a network of new routes full of event, surprise and revelation. It really works at many levels, both physical and mental.

The Magna Trust (client); Billington Structures; Buro Happold; Connell Mott MacDonald; Deacon & Jones, Event Communications; FEDRA; Hyland Edgar Driver; Schal; Speirs and Major Associates

Shown in detail, the strong contrast between contemporary red GRP cladding and the traditional materials of the old steelworks can be seen (main image).

The air pavilion, which takes the form of a dirigible hanging high up in the main space, challenges visitors to enter a unique space by crossing a scary bridge from the central vertical core (far right).

Royal Botanic Gardens Kew London, UK, 2002

Kew Gardens are an extraordinary mixture of scientific institution and picturesque pleasure grounds, in which fine buildings set off one of the world's most extensive and varied plant collections. In the 19th century, the gardens were developed from being a royal enclosure to a public park in which remarkable plants from all over the world could be examined among exquisite garden follies like the Pagoda by William Chambers. In 1848, the Great Palm House designed by Decimus Burton with Richard Turner was opened so that tropical plants, as well as those from temperate climates could be shown to the public. Now restored, this smoothly curved early masterpiece of glass and iron sets a standard for all subsequent building at Kew.

Kew contains the largest plant collection in the world; it remains a first class scientific centre and it has major educational commitments. At the same time, it is a landscape (or rather a series of landscapes) so artistically important that it has been placed on UNESCO's World Heritage List. All these responsibilities need sophisticated co-ordination, and in 2002, Wilkinson Eyre were asked to prepare a development plan for the whole park. It included restoring links with the Thames by reopening vistas and creating a path that winds through the woods on the river bank.

59

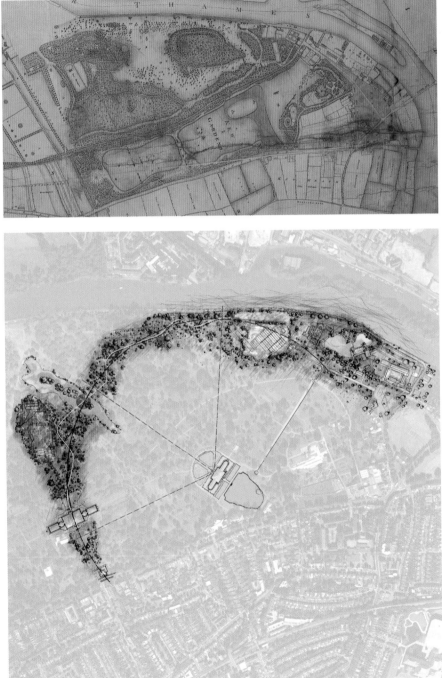

One of the first built results of the plan is the new Alpine House which replaces an aging version that had no effective shading apart from whitewash on the inside of the glass, and in which ventilation did not work properly. Both are vital in the cultivation of alpines, which in their natural state receive abundant quantities of sunlight and are subject to constant air movement at temperatures that never become very hot. As far as possible, the architects were determined to provide such conditions by passive means. At the same time, they wanted to create a building that could live up to the picturesque tradition of Chambers and the innovatory daring of Burton and Turner. (Most of Kew's 20th century buildings are disappointingly utilitarian and dull.)

From the first, it was clear that the building should be tall to ensure that ventilation could work passively by the convection stack effect. Plainly, the house would have to be extensively glazed. And at the same time, it had to be long and thin in plan, so that its short end could be orientated southwards to minimise solar gain. Wilkinson Eyre's solution is based on a pair of double solid steel parabolic arches that span from north to south with a structural spine between them. The maximum height provided by the arches is 10m, and the internal floor area is 96m². To maximise light transmission, the arches use cables inside the glass to support inclined structural glazing on the east and west sides of the building (conventional framed glazing with opening lights covers the spine). On the upper parts of the side walls of the spine, automatically operated pivoting glazing forms the extract for the natural ventilation system. All glazing is in low iron glass, which looks clear rather than green when viewed from its edge; low iron glass combined with silicone joints was tested to give 90% light transmission rather than the 80% offered by standard glass.

Jim Eyre: The setting of the gardens combines a beautiful and historic landscape with numerous listed buildings and structures, of which the Palm House (1848), Pagoda (1762) and Kew Palace (1631) are the key landmarks (far left).

As shown in this part of the Burrell Richardson Plan of 1771, Kew was originally separated in two gardens, physically and philosophically opposed (William Chambers' "town" to Capability Brown's "country"). The legacy needed re-examining to draw people further out into the gardens, while raising awareness of the scientific mission and our interdependence with nature (top right).

The 2002 masterplan by Wilkinson Eyre identified a series of initiatives, generally following an arc rooted in Burton and Nesfield's original geometry, devised to link the gardens. The arc reconnects the gardens to the River Thames (bottom right).

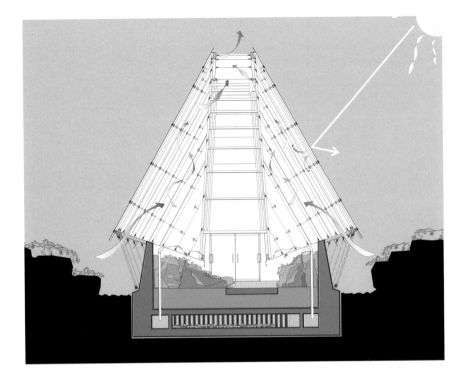

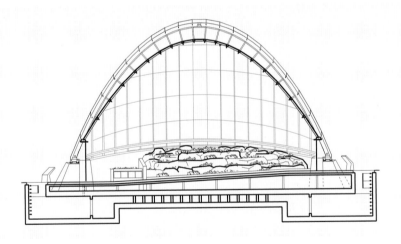

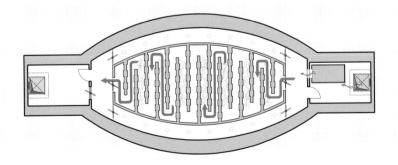

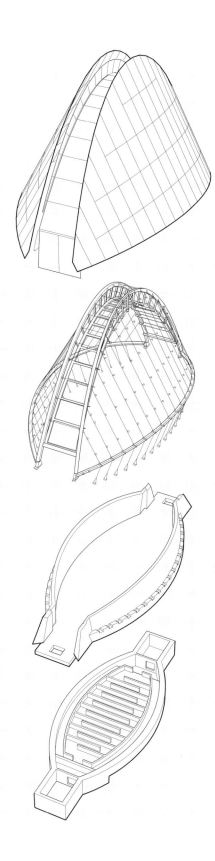

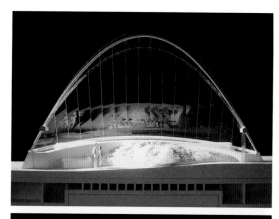

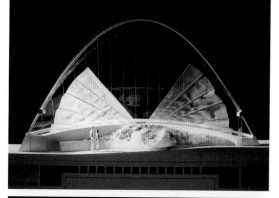

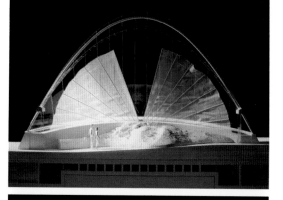

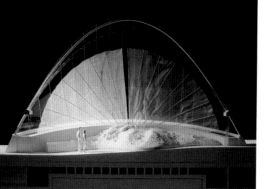

The form is derived from a need to self-ventilate to keep the plants dry and relatively cool, and to provide maximum light levels, particularly during the winter months. The use of paired arches carrying pre-stressed cables allows for very high transparency on the large east and west façades, while minimising exposure to solar gain from the south during the hottest part of the day.

Beneath the house a labyrinth based on the principles of a termite mound in a hot climate provides cool air to be trickled over the plants (left page and near left).

An integral blind system was worked out with a sailmaker to shield the façades when necessary, while increasing the performance of the stack effect ventilation. The sides of the glass house are undercut and are open at low level to allow airflow up to escape at the apex (right).

Air intake is at ground level where air is drawn into the building through a concrete labyrinth that works like a cooling form of hypocaust. At night, cold air is blown through the labyrinth to chill the concrete, while during the day, convection (when necessary mechanically assisted) draws cooled air up to the apex and over the plants. Additional air movement is added by the porches at each end of the spine where the double doors are left open in most weather.

A further source of natural ventilation is assisted by the shading system, a most ingenious, amusing and elegant device. When the sun threatens to overheat the planting beds on each side of the winding path that links the porches, white fabric shades rise inside the glass. Curved aluminium tubes stretch webs of woven polyester fabric into fan-like shapes and, in the void between fans and the glass, convection currents are set up that add to air movements and negate the effects of solar gain.

The Alpine House continues Kew's extraordinarily and continuing civilised culture, which combines science, art, education and commerce. Wilkinson Eyre's new heraldic building, with its precise geometry, finely honed detailing and remarkable climatic control is a proper 21st century successor to the work of Chambers and Burton.

Royal Botanic Gardens Kew (client); Atelier Ten; Chris Blandford Associates (masterplan only); Dewhurst Macfarlane; Fanshawe; Green-Mark International; Killby & Gayford; Tuchschmid Constructa AG

The form and glazing bring a 21st century use of technology to complement the early seminal glasshouses at Kew, light and highly transparent with a finely tuned structure (top left).

The form provides an airy space, a big space for small plants—but still intimate (top right).

Sited on a specific local axis, the house at times is formal in its relationship with the landscape. However, its presence is more generally felt rising from the planting in the foreground or appearing gently in more distant views.

Crystal Palace London, UK, unrealised

For all its importance as a sports centre and the manifold fascinations of its parkland, the site of the Crystal Palace at Sydenham is inevitably touched with melancholy. Joseph Paxton's great building, which had housed the Great Exhibition in 1851, had been moved to South London and enlarged to act as a popular entertainment and arts centre. On 30 November 1936, this magical early triumph of iron and glass building was burned to the ground. It was impossible to rebuild, and has never been replaced in terms of either function or figure.

Wilkinson Eyre's proposal for a sculpture garden and exhibition hall promises to restore much of the site's iconic power, while adding to the mixture of pleasures offered by the park. The main move of the project is a huge 150m long two-storey high oval of glass floating 54m above the trees on the crest of the hill. It hovers precisely over the axis of the transverse aisle of Paxton's palace and becomes a shining landmark on the southern skyline of London—as dramatic and daring an exploration of glass technology in our age as Paxton's great structure was for the Victorians.

69

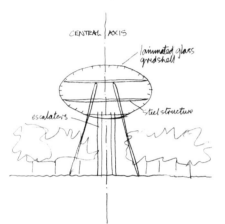

CENTRAL AXIS

laminated glass
gridshell

escalators

steel structure

Chris Wilkinson: When Joseph
Paxton's great Crystal Palace
burned down in 1936, it left
the park in Sydenham without
its main raison d'être or its
important visual landmark
(top left).

Our challenge was to
design a building on a much
smaller scale which could
recreate that necessary visual
presence and reinstate the
important east-west axis that
had previously been set out
along the line of the prominent
transverse aisle of the old
building. This early sketch
shows the concept for the
curvilinear glazed form raised
up above the trees on slender
steel piloti (bottom left).

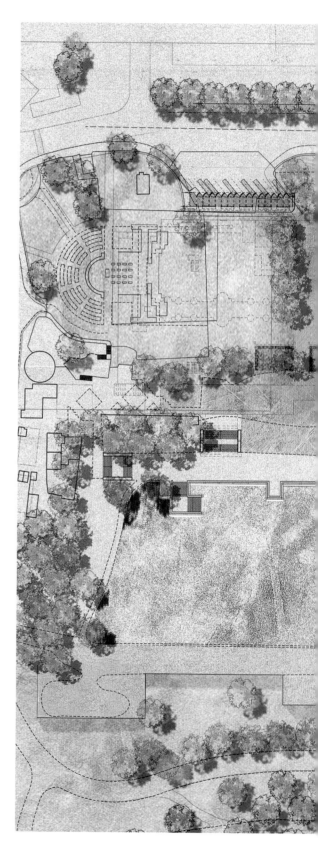

Crystal Palace Parade

sculpture park

Three steel decks are accommodated within the glazed skin, which house plant and service areas on the lowest floor and the main exhibition hall above that, with two large mezzanines at the top accommodating restaurants and bars. The scale of the space is enormous and its geometry is so complex that it couldn't have been set out without the use of the latest 3D computer technology.

Like the Crystal Palace, the new building houses a huge exhibition hall filled with light but, because of its height, commanding wonderful panoramic views over London that the original never had. Terraces at each end of the ovoid enhance the floating experience. The great gallery and its views are reached by the world's longest escalator (though lifts are provided at each end for the impatient and less daring). Two large mezzanines hover above the main floor and house bars and restaurants while below a service level houses kitchens and plant.

Both skin and gridshell structure are of laminated glass, though internal decks are supported by steelwork. The responsive skin of photovoltaic cells encapsulated in glass provides both a source of energy and solar shading (parts of Paxton's building must have been pretty hot on occasion). Ventilation will be by gill-like structures in the underside of the glittering ovoid.

Beneath the hovering gallery is a sculpture garden where, for once, plants have a chance to thrive under a building. As the local residents who commissioned the project hope, the natural landscape will be preserved. They will gain a new cultural centre with unforgettable resonances: it will look like a Martian vehicle from the War of the Worlds peering down over the city; it will be a modern version of the fantastical Victorian dinosaur models in the park; it will be a little brother of Archigram's walking city. And, like the great glass palace, it will be a major London landmark.

Crystal Palace Campaign Committee (client); Arup

Our design for a new exhibition hall pushes glazing technology to the limits in much the same way that Paxton did 150 years earlier. Whilst he pioneered the use of float glass within lightweight framing, we were able to create a laminated glass diagrid structure which supports itself.

The curved form, which occupies the same space as the top part of the transverse aisle of the original structure, stretches 150m across the site to finish in the same position on Crystal Palace Parade as Seurat's famous painting, and the visual impact could well be as dramatic (top images).

Viewed from the park, the new structure appears to float above the trees, providing a vivid contrast with the remaining stone structure of the upper terraces belonging to the old building, whilst from the London Eye, the new Crystal Palace would provide a prominent landmark on the South London skyline (bottom images).

THE PARADE, UPPER NORWOOD.

National Waterfront Museum Swansea, UK, 2005

Wilkinson Eyre have achieved an impressive record in creating buildings which help to regenerate run-down industrial areas. They have made the magical bridge over the Tyne to bring new life to Gateshead and produced schemes like Magna that respond to their physical and cultural contexts to tell the story of past wonders. The work has proved popular and has clearly helped to energise local economies. One of the latest of such projects to be completed is the National Waterfront Museum at Swansea's South Dock.

77

The city was one of the key centres of the Industrial Revolution because it was close to the easily worked coal seams that acquired great importance after the discovery of methods of smelting ore using coal were invented in the mid-17th century. Just across the Bristol Channel in Cornwall were large copper deposits but no coal, and it proved sensible to bring copper ore over the Channel to be smelted in the Tawe Valley (the smelting process required four or five tons of coal for each ton of copper ore, so the economics of location were obvious).

By the mid-19th century, the valley had a dozen smelters and was nicknamed Copperopolis. It had to cater for so much sea traffic that new handling facilities were needed, and Swansea's South Dock was completed in 1859. Its original commercial functions have now completely disappeared, so the north side of the dock has became a perfect site for the new National Waterfront Museum which is intended to be a catalyst for regeneration of the old Maritime Quarter—a link between Swansea bay and the city centre. One large quayside building remained, Shed 21, a spare two-storey brick structure built in 1900 to handle general cargo, and was then converted into the home of the Swansea Maritime and Industrial Museum (SMIM). It and its floating exhibits have now been incorporated into the National Waterfront Museum.

Chris Wilkinson: The 1875 ordnance survey map revealed that the site had previously been covered by a criss-crossing arrangement of railway lines which have long since disappeared. Each one of these lines has now been reinstated into the building or landscape in some way, enhancing the contextual memory. This early sketch masterplan attempts to express some of this geometry of past uses on the site (top).

The layout responds to three site-related geometries: the orthogonal line of the existing warehouse along the dockside; the angular direct route to the market square in the centre of Swansea; and the arcing line of the old railway revetment wall which used to traverse the site. The resultant complex form of the three connected geometries enriches the architecture with an underlying narrative which may or may not be understood by the visitor (bottom).

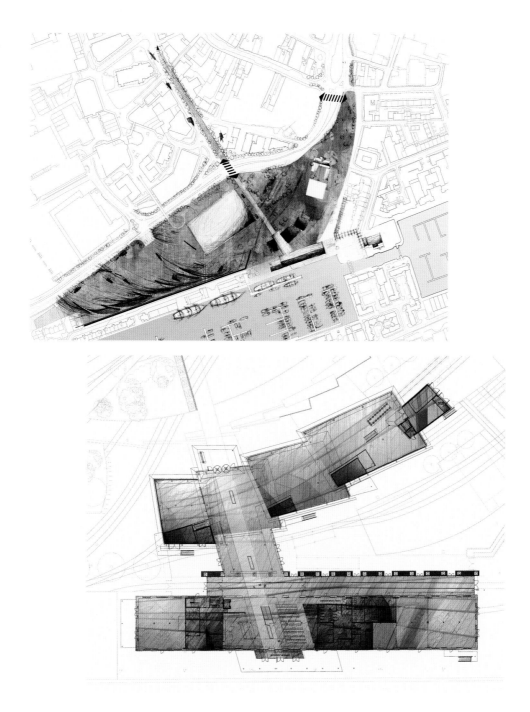

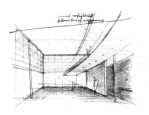

GALLERIES WITH 2 GEOMETRIES

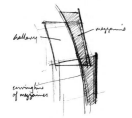

The new galleries are composed of four rotating, interlocking rhomboid forms which increase in size in the same proportion as their rotation. There is no magic formula for this, but it just seems right (left).

The sketches explore the relationship between the curved mezzanine, expressing the line of the railway within the parallelogram form of the gallery (far left).

The intervention of the new link building with the historic warehouse manifests itself on the waterfront with a projecting cantilevered roof canopy and viewing terrace (bottom left and bottom right).

This image (top right) shows the contrasting elevational treatments between the punctured opening of the south wall and the curtain walling of the west wall.

Exploring the site, the architects were struck by the way in which remaining fragments of railway tracks revealed the dynamics of the defunct industrial port. They decided to reinstate and reinforce these traces in their new landscape and within the old building and cause the new work to follow the curve of the revetment wall which used to support a high-level track to the quayside. The curve turns towards the Royal Institution, an 1839 building that has also been turned into a museum, so there is hope that a future extension will lock the whole museum quarter together. Striking across the curve is a pedestrian axis that connects the city centre with the waterfront through the new range and the existing SMIM building. Intersection of curve and axis provides the formal entrance to the complex. A glazed link on the axis forms a foyer joining old and new. The axis culminates in the museum's café and shop that overlook the waterfront and harbour basin. A large void has been cut into the first floor of the 100 year old building to unite old and new spatially and bring light down to the café. A stair runs up to an observation platform and the first floor gallery where, under the exposed roof structure, neutral spaces can be used for exhibition or education. Part of the ground floor of the old building is devoted to administration and museological services, but the rest is given over to commercial uses: cafés, bars and shops, which will bring life back to the waterfront.

Under the projecting flat roof, a simple repetitive cladding module incorporates varying horizontal bands, with transparent glazing in the top clerestory and at the base. The middle band varies in opacity from clear at the entrance to translucent for the main galleries and completely opaque for the "future" gallery at the west end. This photograph shows the transition from day to night, emphasising this varying opacity (top).

The south elevation of the interlocking new galleries is clad with three different types of local Welsh slate bonded to large prefabricated concrete panels. This is a response to environmental issues—the need to reduce daylight in the spaces behind—and also forms an important part of the building's narrative (bottom).

In the new building, the three interlocking galleries and the entrance that constitute the curve are rhomboidal in plan; each rotates and increases in size in proportion of 1:1·2 to its neighbour to generate the overall plan form. The two easterly galleries are connected by a curved mezzanine, allowing for the dramatic display of objects of very different size, illumination and scale in a similar way to Wilkinson Eyre's provision for exhibiting similar heterogeneous objects in the Making the Modern World Gallery of the Science Museum in London. Externally, the curve has two completely different expressions. To the north, structural glazing (continuous transoms with stainless steel rods for mullions) admits copious quantities of light to the galleries.

The south side is clad in slate with only a few heavily shaded slit openings. The slate is a celebration of the Welsh national mineral, three types of which are bonded to large prefabricated concrete panels and arranged on edge in strips, the depth of which is determined by the natural limitations of quarried slate. The strips are separated by thin bands of aluminium to provide sparkle. North and south sides are united visually by continuing the proportions of the slate bands in the glass. But the north elevation is a negative of the south, with dark aluminium transom strips in place of the sparkling ones, and milky white glass taking the role of slate on the south side.

A close-up interior view of the cladding shows the transparency of the lower level enhanced by having the curtain walling hung from the structure above (top images).

Contrasting exhibition space has been created in the spectacular interior of the existing building (centre left).

Interior views of the new galleries before and after fit-out show their capacity to house large objects from the museum's collection (bottom right).

No museum built today can possibly ignore sustainability: the building itself must become an exhibit showing how to construct with proper care for the planet. Measures used in Swansea range from the restoration of the existing building and regeneration of a grey site blasted by industry and its aftermath to careful selection of local skills and materials —for instance, the slate, steel, stone and glass are all Welsh. The almost imperforate south wall of the new galleries is clearly a device to avoid solar gain, but other less obvious energy-saving devices include grey water recycling, solar collectors and use of the harbour waters as a heat sink.

Such environmental messages are not the only ones the building has to convey. By drawing on the original industrial geometry of the site, the history of the place is evoked. Welsh materials and local skills are expressions of the country's continuing industrial abilities. By reinvigorating the waterfront, Swansea is reminded of its amazingly successful trading history, and the past is brought into discussion with the present, both commercially and intellectually. These juxtapositions are emphasised and orchestrated by the building itself, with its contrasts of light and dark, opaque and translucent, old and new. Unlike Magna, the Swansea building simply alludes to the narrative of past uses on the site through its spatial organisation and key physical references. Combining new and old provides an evocative yet flexible series of sets on which the curators can mount their own dramas.

National Waterfront Museum Swansea (client); Arup; Davis Langdon; Land Design Studio; McCann & Partners; Mowlem South Wales

The slate wall was constructed of 40mm thick pieces of slate in a variety of widths, bonded to precast concrete panels and hoisted in 6m bays. Three different kinds of slate from three different local Welsh quarries provide a variety of colours. They are set out in apparently random bands within a module of different heights which carries round into the glazed cladding on the other elevations (top).

Narrow slot windows through the slate wall with opaque glass brise-soleil allow natural light into the space without solar gain. The planar slate walls are lifted off the ground with a recessed area set just above head height playing tricks with the perceived scale (bottom).

The solidity of the planar wall to the south of the new galleries contrasts vividly with the fully glazed north wall (following pages, right).

Hélène Binet's night shot of the north façade emphasises its transparency, in comparison with the solidity of the south façade (following pages).

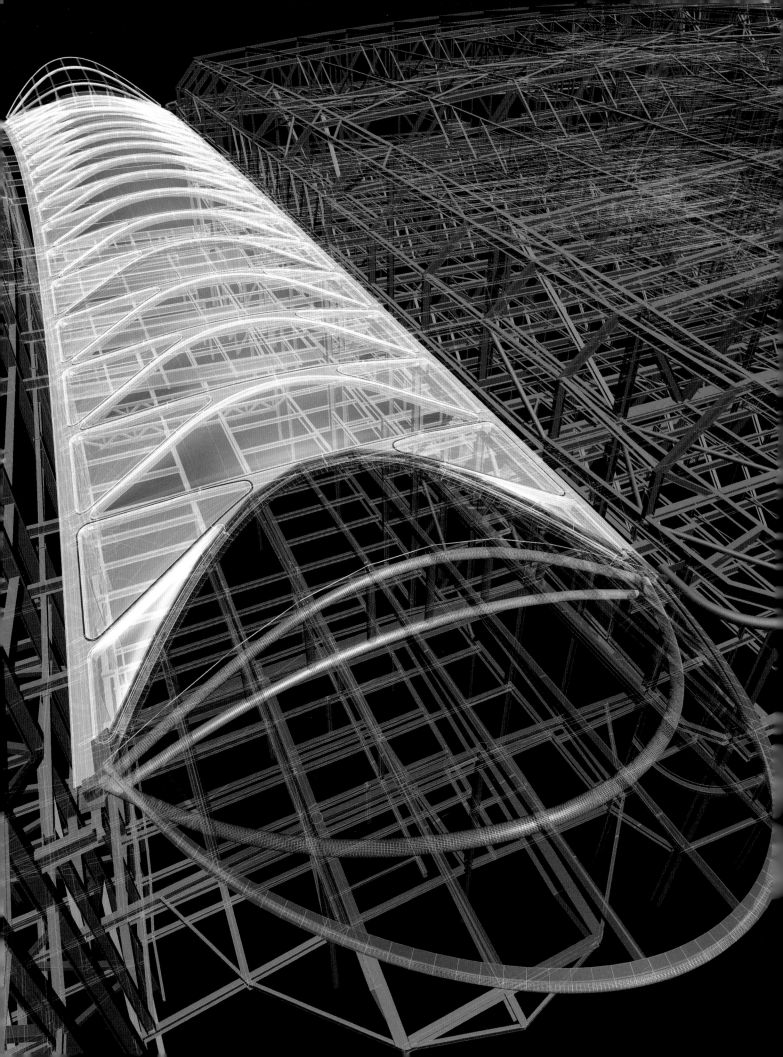

Liverpool was voted to be European City of Culture in 2008, intensifying a need for new public buildings. Wilkinson Eyre won the international design competition for new civic facilities, including a multi-purpose arena with capacity for an audience of 9,500, a 1,350 seat auditorium and an exhibition hall. These are supported by a multi-storey car park, a couple of hotels and some housing.

The site is one of the most important in the city: King's Waterfront, on the Mersey south-west of the centre and just south of the Albert Dock is lined by wonderfully stern brick warehouses, fine enough to be on UNESCO's World Heritage list. For better or worse, by the time of the competition, everything on King's Waterfront had been razed and its docks filled in, so Wilkinson Eyre were presented with a huge platform overlooking the vast expanse of the estuary and its ever-changing light.

Chris Wilkinson: The new Arena and Convention Centre takes its place on the famous Mersey Waterfront to the south of the listed Albert Docks. Its low, horizontal form allows clear views of the Anglican and Roman Cathedrals behind (top).

The design has been carried out in 3D from the start of the process, which has led to a sculptural form related to the individual functions. The rendered section shows the form of the arena with its raked seating built into the piazza, complemented by a similar form containing the convention centre with its 1,350 seat auditorium and breakout spaces located above the exhibition hall. These two main forms are connected by the galleria, which is the "hinge" of the development (bottom).

Arenas and auditoria are notoriously problematic to accommodate in a coherent urban fabric, almost as difficult as multi-storey car parks. The architects had to make civic sense out of what would normally be a collection of individual object buildings. They decided to use a glazed galleria to connect the biggest element, the arena, to a similar block containing auditorium and exhibition hall arranged to form a conference centre; roofs of the two blocks are arranged like the shells of an opened bivalve with the galleria as hinge. The base of the U-shaped bowl of the arena is dramatically exposed to a concourse at entrance level, and the whole is wrapped in a glazed circulation zone that connects to the galleria and reveals the massive volume of the arena hovering above. In the southern shell, the big auditorium has two revolving banks of seats so it can be transformed rapidly into three separate smaller independent spaces. Meeting and breakout spaces are arranged round the edge to catch the light and offer views out over the city and river and down into the galleria.

The roofs of the auditorium and arena are double curved. Their shapes would not have been possible to achieve without three-dimensional digital technology. New in both shape and scale, their forms were honed to allow them to be set out and constructed as simply as possible. Anodised aluminium rain screens cover the curving roof forms and wrap over the eaves to connect to the walls. These are formed of two distinct bands of glazing which are intended to break down the scale of the huge complex. The lower band is of transparent vertical panes, while the upper layer is inclined to meet the aluminium eaves and has a geometric fritted pattern.

In plan, the U-shaped 9,500 seat arena is linked to the convention centre by a glazed galleria which connects with the new public piazza to the east and the Mersey waterfront in the west. The piazza is further contained by a multi-storey car park and a pair of hotels to the east (right).

94

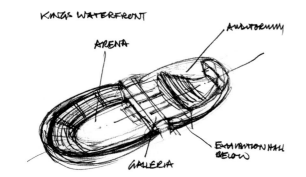

KINGS WATERFRONT
ARENA
AUDITORIUM
GALLERIA
EXCAVATION HALL BELOW

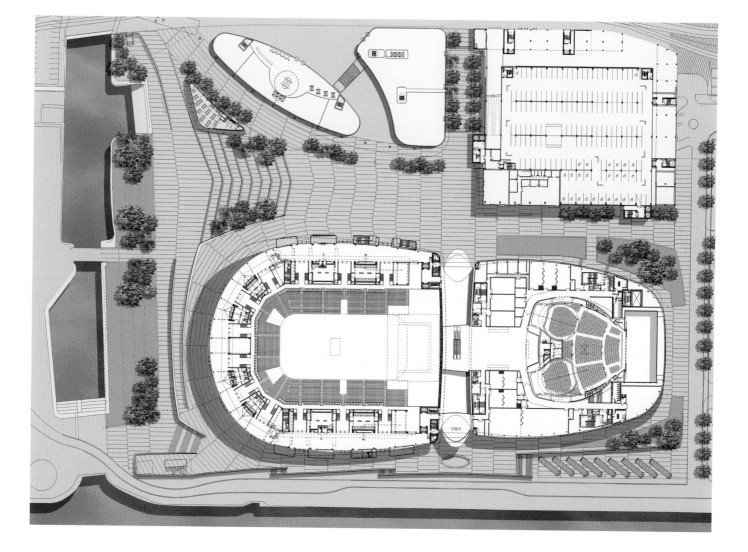

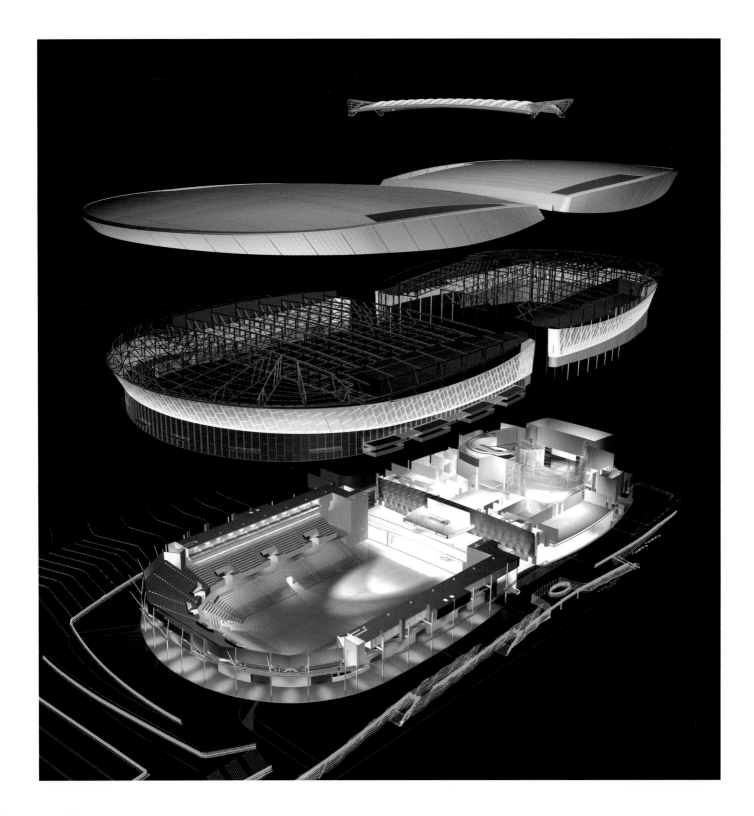

The galleria, which is filled with light from its transparent roof of ETFE pillows supported on cross-vaulted steel, sets up an east-west axis across the site that is continued on the landward side by an avenue between the car park in the south-east quadrant of the site and the hotels in the north-east. Sheltered from the prevailing south-west winds by these two blocks and the continuous line of the arena and conference centre is a generous piazza which will have shops, cafes and restaurants at ground level along the edges of the hotel complex and the north and west faces of the multi-storey car park. Above retail level on these sides, the parking building will be clad in stainless steel mesh to allow for ventilation and give an appearance of solidity. The south and east fronts of this normally scaleless and antiurban type of building are to be wrapped in single aspect housing.

The architects have been concerned to relate new to old. From the Mersey, it is clear that the site is a vital element in the cityscape. In plan, it forms the riverside end of a visual axis that terminates on the high ridge above the city in the charged gap between the Catholic and the Anglican cathedrals that dominate the city centre and form a backdrop to the waterfront. One reason for conjoining arena and conference centre was precisely to link the two distant cathedrals into a coherent cityscape. In another gesture to the existing urban structure, the hotels in the north-east corner of the piazza are curved in plan to allow visual connections with the city centre.

The composition of the curvilinear shell makes a strong architectural statement on the waterfront. This exploded image of the 3D model shows the complexity of the various elements, which have been moulded through a process similar to product design to create a unique, sculptural and coherent form (opposite page).

Landscaping (evolved with Gustafson Porter) aims to preserve and enhance fragments from the past, such as the King's Waterfront quayside with its bollards and massive masonry. The main aim of the landscape plan is to provide flowing surfaces to link the disparate elements of the complex, and to provide smooth transition between levels (entrances to the arena and conference centre are 3m above quayside level, and the building is sunk by an equal amount to create a services level under the piazza). As part of the city's policy of making the complex accessible to as many people as possible by offering a wide range of activities, an open air theatre and a skating rink are integrated into the hard landscape.

The variety of the landscape is an echo of the variety of the whole complex, which will surely reanimate this disjunctive urban quarter. It will add to the great sweep of waterfront activities from the Three Graces (monumental Edwardian commercial buildings), past fine dock buildings (now art galleries, shops and apartments) to the multifarious uses of the cultural area. The whole area will be regenerated and linked organically to the city centre. The huge project is currently on site and is due to open for New Year's celebrations in 2008.

Liverpool City Council (client); Bovis Lend Lease; Buro Happold; Faber Maunsell; Gleeds; Gustafson Porter; Sandy Brown Associates; Speirs and Major Associates; Sport Concepts; Theatre Projects Consultants

This aerial view of the development, as seen from the city, shows the new piazza protected from the prevailing winds by the arena and hotels, and stepping down towards Duke's Dock (main image).

A rendered view of the galleria shows the vaulted roof infilled with ETFE pillow fabric covering the main space, and connection between all the different activities at all levels (top).

This important regeneration project for Liverpool's City of Culture in 2008 will help to draw people down to an enlivened waterfront, with activities over several levels of terraces. With construction under way, the scale of the development can be appreciated (left and right).

"Bridge of Aspiration" London, UK, 2003

Floral Street is a tall, narrow thoroughfare in Covent Garden, distinguished at its east end by the side of the great mid-19th century mass of E. M. Barry's Royal Opera House. Across the street from Barry's impassive neo-Classical façade is the new Royal Ballet School and, as part of the Opera House's extensive revitalisation programme, it was decided to link it to the school with a pedestrian bridge over the street at fourth floor level. Apparently wilful, Wilkinson Eyre's extraordinary design is in fact a remarkably imaginative and daring response to a complicated set of geometric and programmatic problems.

103

Floor heights in the two buildings are different, so the bridge had to slope downwards from the school towards Barry's building. At the same time, it had to shift from left to right in plan for functional reasons and the need to make as little impact as possible on the façade of the Opera House (which is listed Grade I). A further difficulty was added by the need to prefabricate the bridge to minimise disruption in the street and reduce problems of construction in such an inaccessible place.

In response to the shifts in axis and the differing levels, it was decided to generate a twisted structure that could meet school and Opera House neatly and orthogonally at each end. Yet the structure had to be as simple as possible. A single but geometrically complex aluminium box beam carries all the loads. The twist is imparted by a series of 24 square oak and aluminium portals, each rotated by four degrees relative to its neighbours, giving the whole a quarter turn as it crosses the street. Between the portals are plane strips of silicon-bonded float glass in which the outer layer is heat-strengthened and the inner one toughened; a clear PVB interlayer joins the two. On two sides, the glass is translucent to prevent overlooking of neighbouring residential property from the bridge and to provide privacy for the dancers as they cross the street.

Jim Eyre: Initial investigations experimented with the idea of incorporating a twisting profile in order to exploit rather than suffer the effects of rake and skew on what might otherwise be rectilinear organisation to the elevations (top).

A rapid evolution occurred with the thought that a series of square frames which, all at once raking, skewing and twisting, could follow the direction of movement across the bridge (bottom left).

After a simple check to verify that the rotating squares would not be too large yet still allow sufficient space for users, the core principles of the concept immediately became apparent. Incidentally, this was the only phase in the design and fabrication process which was not digitally enabled (bottom right).

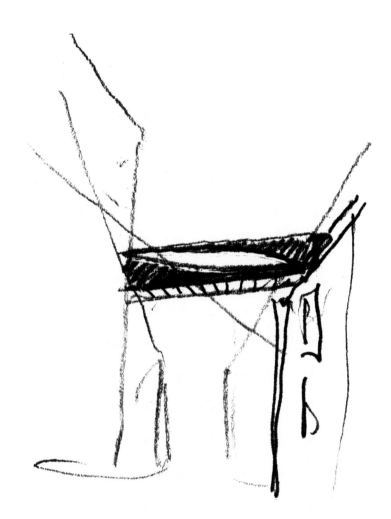

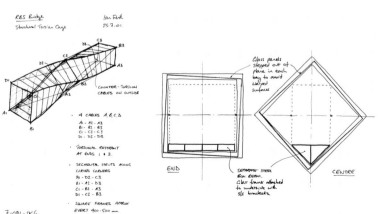

RBS Bridge

Ian Firth

Structural Torsion Cage

25.7.01.

COUNTER - TORSION
CABLES ON OUTSIDE

• 4 CABLES A,B,C,D
  A1 - A2 - A3
  B1 - B2 - B3
  C1 - C2 - C3
  D1 - D2 - D3

• TORSIONAL RESTRAINT
  AT ENDS 1 & 3.

• SEGMENTAL STRUTS ALONG
  CURVED CORNERS
  A1 - D2 - C3
  B1 - A2 - D3
  C1 - B2 - A3
  D1 - C2 - B3

• SQUARE FRAMES APPROX
  EVERY 400-500 mm

7-091-SK6

Glass panels
stepped out of
plane in each
bay to avoid
warped
surfaces

END

Separate steel
box beam.
Glass frames attached
to underside with
s/s brackets.

CENTRE

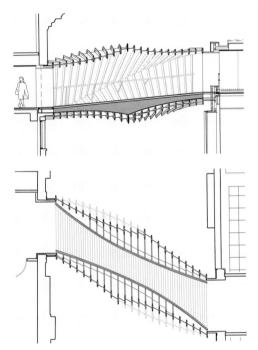

Use of different kinds of glass (transparent and diffuse) also makes the twisting form clear from a distance. At night, the bridge is lit by LED fittings integrated into the mullions that bring out the rhythm and curves of the structure (and are incidentally cheap and reliable in use). In winter, the hollow beam acts as plenums for supply and return ventilation, with fresh air being warmed by fan-coil heater units under the floor. On sunny days, solar heat gain is moderated by the timber profiles of the portals.

Inside, the floor slopes gently down to the Opera House, enclosed by the magical spiralling curves of the walls that, however sensuous, are of course rigorously composed of straight elements. Crossing the street, no-one can be unmoved by the bridge's elegant sense of movement that is occasioned by a most imaginative interpretation of the geometrical complexities of the site. The school has called it the "Bridge of Aspiration," and Amanda Moxey, their Communication and Marketing Manager, says that "I feel uplifted every time I cross the bridge: it makes my day." Externally, the delicate light structure (which was lifted and secured in place in a couple of hours one Sunday morning) is a mysterious dancing presence, totally original and metaphoric of the institutions it serves. From both inside and out, the bridge is a surprise: you enter it from nondescript spaces in the buildings and suddenly find yourself floating in luminance over the narrow street; looking up from below, you see a totally unexpected shimmering crystal, twisting against the sky.

Royal Ballet School (client); Buro Happold; Flint & Neill Partnership; GIG Fassadenbau GmbH; Speirs and Major Associates

The simplicity and close "fit" of the concept belies the complexity of the task in establishing a precise definition of the geometry. Every turn of every frame must capture the edges of the glazing in between the mullions, and even minor adjustments arising out of surveys and development of details required the entire geometry to be re-cast. As revealed in the section it was opportune that the geometric residue of depth occurred mid-span where structurally necessary, while allowing the slenderest profiles to meet the abutments (top left).

The related narrowing of the walking surface in plan somehow accentuates the sense of a high crossing (bottom left).

Night and day views show how lighting, fully integrated into the mullions, and the use of contrasting materials of oak and aluminium act to reinforce the visual definition of the twisting geometry—making a "balletic" space (main images).

The totally hidden beam occupying the space sub-floor is something of a tour de force of folded aluminium plates held, analogous to yacht hull construction, in a series of scantlings (bottom left).

The completion of this beam allowed the entire bridge to be assembled (fully glazed) off site and delivered and installed in a morning (top left).

In the canyon that is Floral Street the twisting form high up above is akin to a chance encounter that might quicken the pulse, while internally it is intended that users experience a metaphorical moment of dancing from the labyrinth of one building to the other (left and following pages).

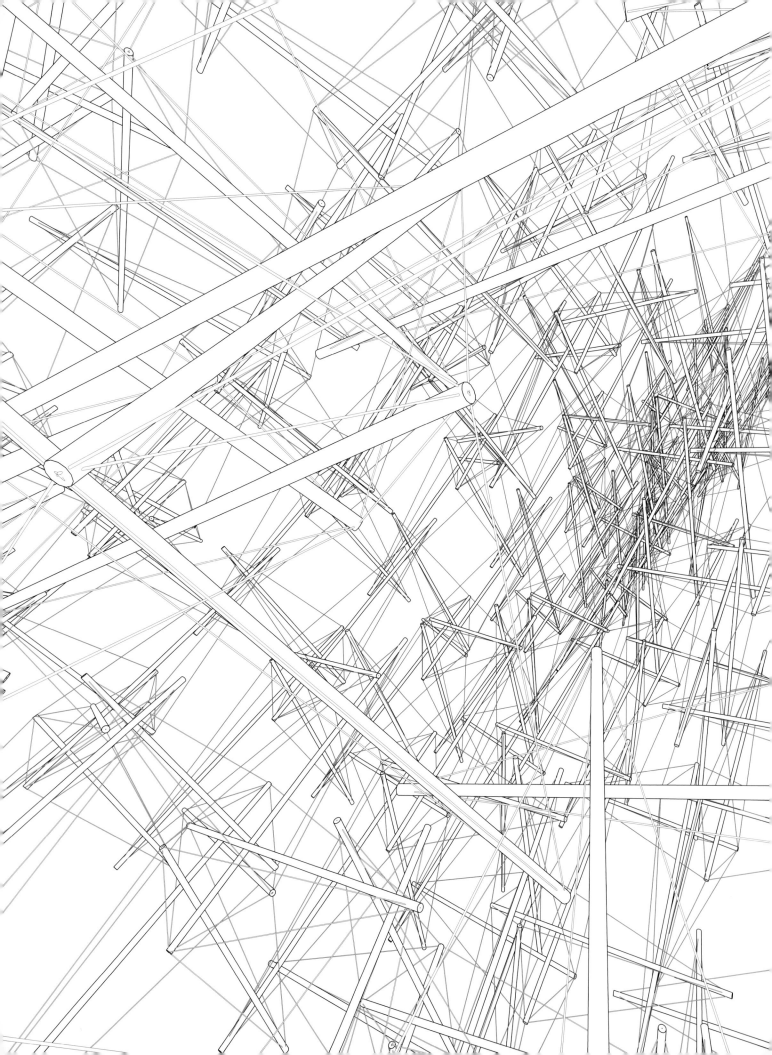

Tensegrity Bridge Washington DC, USA, unrealised

The most ethereal of Wilkinson Eyre's bridge proposals is a project for the National Building Museum in Washington DC. Like the architects' 1997 bridge in the London Science Museum which elegantly demonstrates structural principles and the properties of materials by responding to imposed stresses with electronic sounds, the Washington bridge will demonstrate tension and compression by responding with light.

Montgomery Meigs finished his massive brick Pension Building in 1887. It was built to process the huge number of pensions that had to be paid to Civil War veterans. When that function became obsolete, it was occupied by other government agencies and the huge Great Hall was used for state functions like banquets and presidential inaugural balls. In 1980, it was converted into the National Building Museum (though its ceremonial functions continue).

113

The Tensegrity Bridge is intended to span from balcony to balcony across the Great Hall at second floor (third level). It is to be a three-dimensional mesh, strong but lightweight, so that its presence will not detract from the great volume Meigs created. In an elongated tetrahedral shape, a series of tensegrity modules is combined to create spaces within the structure to allow people to walk through it. As the architects say, the bridge is intended to have "volume without sheer opaque mass;" it will have presence, hovering over the dancers and diners without preventing them from sometimes gazing up into the dark void beyond.

The contrast between space defined by heavy 19th century masonry and volume sketched in lightweight modern materials will be made clear because the 2m long tubular polycarbonate compressive elements of the great structure will be lit up with light emitting diodes, which during the day will continually alter their pattern of illumination, responding to the changing stresses put on the structure by people walking across the transparent deck.

Prototypes, such as the one exhibited at the 2004 Venice Biennale, have shown that such a poetic fusion of art, architecture and engineering will work, and that it has a powerful, if diaphanous presence. On a large scale, this instructive and beautiful art installation could be magical.

National Building Museum (client); Arup

Jim Eyre: The assembly behaves as a structural sponge, soaking up force, and as an exhibit by each compression member illuminating to display its varying loads as people move over the bridge. An ambiguity between architecture, exhibition design and art installation demonstrates a relaxing of boundaries between disciplines (right).

114

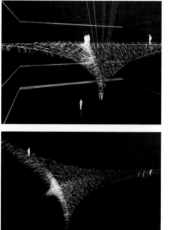

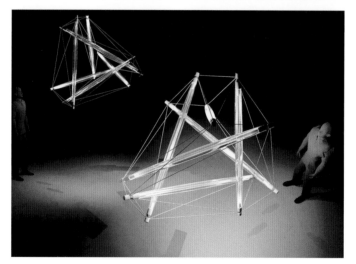

The objective was to combine both lightness as appropriate to the bridge with visual mass. A minimal structure would have become lost in the extraordinary scale of the museum's internal court (top left).

The initial ideas evolved around a cloud of small structural members, later rationalised with Cecil Balmond into a cellular system of tensegrity modules achieving the same variation in density of members as originally sought (bottom left).

A model of the structure was made in the office and displayed as part of the practice's "Reflections" installation in the Italian Pavilion at the 2004 Venice Architecture Biennale (right).

Schools for the Future various locations, 2003–

The Government Department for Education and Skills (DfES) asked a number of inventive practices to produce designs for secondary schools that could act as models for future development, capable of adaptation by other architects on a wide variety of sites. Wilkinson Eyre made a proposal for one of these "exemplar schools" in which key elements of the building type are standardised so that they can be arranged in an almost limitless variety of configurations, according to topography, orientation, access and local demand (the schools are intended to serve the whole community, not only people of school age).

Wilkinson Eyre's analysis led them to producing a kit of parts with three basic forms of accommodation: learning clusters, central facilities (housing particular services and not necessarily physically central to the plan), all linked by an agora or common space. Learning clusters can cater for between 220 to 300 students and act almost as schools within the whole school; they are intended to give pupils a sense of individual place, communality and security. Depending on individual schools' policies, the clusters can be used to accommodate learning villages, departmental specialisms, house groups or year groups. The clusters are wedge-shaped in plan with the short side providing access and connection to the agora. Long sides are made up of rows of classrooms of adjustable length (width remains standard). These look out on the surrounding landscape and are reached through the central double-height, top-lit triangular volume that contains IT learning resources. The area at the apex of each wedge can have an outdoor terrace for teaching and recreation, or provide a double-height space for other activities such as art. At the opposite end, the staff room is positioned to survey both the entrance and the central space. Stairs, lift and lavatories are also adjacent to the entrance.

119

Each school's central facilities are housed in more conventional orthogonal blocks. An assembly building offers facilities for music and drama as well as gathering; the sport building is not only a gym, but doubles as the school's dance centre. Similarly, the one-storey dining block can be quickly adapted for other uses. Of all the central facilities, the reception building is the one most visited by students and visitors alike: it contains a counter facing the agora with a general office and administrative space behind.

The agora is the tissue that binds all the elements together; unlike the learning clusters and central facilities, the agora has no predetermined shape. Its shape is determined by the nature of the site and possibilities of extension (additional learning clusters are to be anticipated in most cases). Wilkinson Eyre's initial proposals show either a large open central area (like a traditional agora) with peripheral buildings connected by covered ways and bridges, or a sinuous, glazed and heated street-like space connecting the learning clusters, with central facilities located at each end of the internal thoroughfare. In most cases the agora will be open to the general public for fairs and events, and it will give evening and weekend access to, for instance, the assembly or sports buildings. Smart cards and electronic gates could ensure that only staff and students could get into the learning clusters and administrative areas.

Chris Wilkinson: Our research into educational needs and buildability requirements during the exemplar project led to the design of a series of components based around the two-storey learning clusters, affectionately known as "strawberries" because of their shape, arranged around an "agora" space linking the learning clusters and general facilities buildings. The idea stems from the traditional cloistered courtyard system which provides covered access to the outsides of buildings rather than internal corridors (main image).

Internally, the learning cluster can be arranged in a number of ways. At the John Madejski Academy in Reading, two standard two-storey clusters support the secondary school while a single-storey cluster provides for a severe learning difficulties unit. At Bristol, we have incorporated differing layouts to provide a mixture of open-plan and more traditional classroom space (bottom).

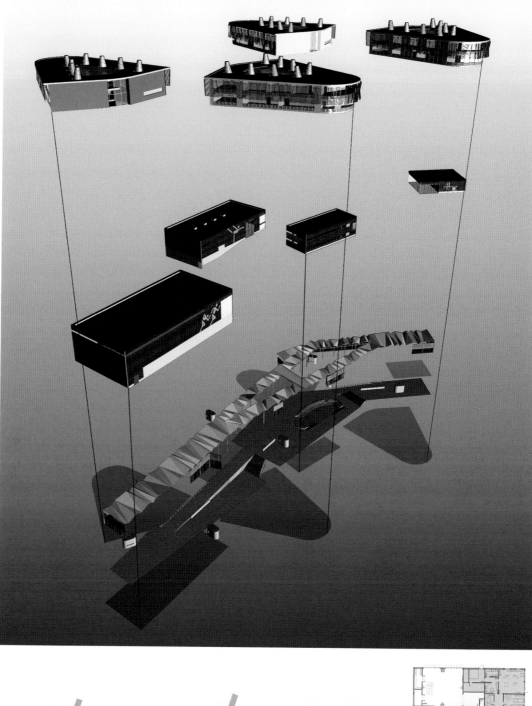

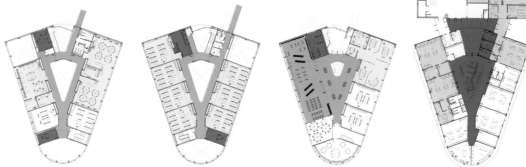

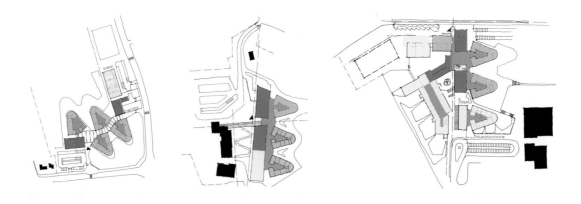

One of the aims of the design is to achieve good environmental performance with passive systems and small expenditure of power. With the exception of IT server rooms, there is no artificial cooling. Space heating is from a wood-fed boiler and water is warmed in roof-top solar collectors. Natural ventilation is organised to avoid noise spreading from one room to another, with classrooms separately linked to rooftop ventilators.

During the day in summer, all vents are opened, and air is drawn through the building by the stack effect and led out through the roof ventilators. Excessive solar gain is avoided by external louvres. On summer nights, the vents remain open and cool air is drawn over the concrete ceiling slabs cooling them, so that they can absorb heat during the day. In winter, the louvres allow sunlight to penetrate the interior. Fresh air is drawn into classrooms via trickle vents and warmed by radiators. At night, all windows and vents are closed, and the well-sealed and highly insulated building maintains even temperatures by means of heat gained during the day.

The DfES has backed the proposal, and the first of the Wilkinson Eyre schools is the John Madejski Academy, being built in south Reading. The architects developed the design to suit the specific curriculum demands of the Academy using the elements evolved in the theoretical study. Its open site allows the four learning clusters to look out onto grass and trees. The agora is a generous informal space, designed with places for informal teaching and events as well as casual encounter. It is entirely covered with single foil ETFE held taught between steel trusses by spring loaded stainless steel cables.

The kit of parts school design has proved popular with education authorities, and there are a number of schools currently under construction which use the system in varying forms. The John Madejski Academy was the first project commissioned, and its four learning clusters are constructed with a reinforced concrete frame and arranged to suit the site configuration (main image and top left).

At Whitefield Fishponds Community School, the clusters are set out in a straight line, spaced away from a rectangular block of general facilities with a heated agora space (top middle). At Hartcliffe Education Campus the configuration is completely different to suit the requirements of a "through school," accommodating children from nursery level through to the sixth form (top right).

Its glazed arcade winds sinuously through the landscape to ensure that each of the other elements of the organisation can enjoy optimum orientation to the landscape in which much design effort has been invested. A new mound around the south side of the school complex moderates traffic noise and encloses social and outdoor teaching areas. A ha-ha on the north side of the building and along the main sports pitch defines further outdoor teaching areas and, planted with reeds and irises, becomes a biological study area. It is crossed by small timber bridges connecting to the sports fields (the school's sponsor John Madejski has made sport one of the main emphases of the curriculum). The place will be fully open in autumn 2007, when the ideas will be tested in reality for the first time.

In the meantime, the concept has proved so popular that it is being used in another two secondary schools, in Bristol at Whitefield and Hartcliffe. The proposals explore different configurations of elements related to particular sites and demonstrate the flexibility of the kit. Unlike the British school building systems of the 1960s and 1970s, the kit will be applicable to a variety of school types, in some ways like the contemporaneous Californian School Construction Systems Development, which did not require huge national bureaucratic ordering and manufacturing programmes, but could be applied to programmes large and small and sites of the most diverse kinds.

Exemplar Schemes: DfES (client); Arup; Davis Langdon

John Madejski Academy: DfES/John Madejski (client); Arup; Buro Four; Costain; Davis Langdon; Grant Associates; Tribal Group

Bristol Schools: Bristol City Council/Skanska (client); Arup; Buro Happold; Grant Associates

The John Madejski Academy is one of the first Building Schools for the Future (BSF) projects to go on site, and these construction images clearly show the distinctive central atrium space within one of the clusters, which can be used for a variety of learning activities (opposite).

King's Cross Gas Holders London, UK, concept stage

The old marshalling yards behind King's Cross station have been one of the worst physical scandals of London since the end of the Second World War. For decades, attempts have been made to produce schemes to urbanise the area that has been full of seedy uses, totally inappropriate for the middle of a great city. All attempts have failed so far because of planning problems, financial setbacks or a combination of both. Now at last the whole area is being transformed by the imminent arrival of the Channel Tunnel Rail link at St Pancras station (the neighbour of King's Cross), and the developer Argent has a proposal for the old goods yard which has been accepted by the planning authorities. Resources to back the proposal are available, and at last the wasteland may become a lively and urbane part of inner London.

Among the few remaining interesting structures marooned amid mounds of rubble are four Victorian gas holders, the support structures of which became the landmark for the area. Once gas holders (or gasometers) were widely known throughout the land, for they were needed as storage vessels by local coal-gas companies, but North Sea gas made them unnecessary. The King's Cross group was one of the very few left in the country, and though the gas cylinders had long ceased to rise and fall with the volume of gas they contained, their supporting cast and wrought iron structures became a memorable landmark for the deserted area. They were listed by the government as Grade II historic buildings, so ensuring their periodical painting and survival.

127

Under the Argent scheme, the support structures will be moved and changed in function. They will be part of an east-west strip of renewed 19th and 20th century industrial buildings hard by the St Pancras canal basin. Wilkinson Eyre's scheme for re-using the circular Victorian cages will see their transformation into frames for residential cylinders that visually will take the place of the massive gas holders. Three of the towers will be clustered as before, with the fourth nearby. In the centre of the cluster will be a virtual cylinder, a volume created by taking a bite out of each of the surrounding forms to make a private open space in the middle of the group. External cladding will be glass, fritted with a pattern derived from an 1880s gas holder.

Top-lit atria in the middle of the larger towers will allow the flats to have double aspect. At ground level will be cafés, bars and shops serving the surrounding urbane pedestrianised spaces. Other public facilities will include a restaurant on the top of the tallest tower which will project above its surrounding metal structure, and the fourth (detached) tower that will contain a variety of public uses yet to be decided. Walkways at the top of the Victorian work will link the three towers, which will have roof-top gardens to provide splendid views of central London, of which the scheme will by then be an integral part.

Argent (client); Arup; Davis Langdon; Faber Maunsell; Speirs and Major Associates; Townshend Associates

Chris Wilkinson: The King's Cross gas holders have long been recognised as an important landmark on the hinterland of run-down railway sidings behind the station (top left).

Wilkinson Eyre won a competition held by the developers Argent to construct a series of apartment buildings within the retained cast iron structures. The concept, as shown in these sketches, is for three cylinders of accommodation, linked by a fourth cylinder which is cut out as a void. This deals with the problem of the complex junction of the cast iron triplet and provides a central landscaped open space as an amenity for the dwellings. Each block of accommodation varies in height as a reference back to the rise and fall of the gasometer enclosures. One peeps out above the structure to provide a restaurant with panoramic views and another is kept low to accommodate a rooftop garden (bottom left).

At night, the fourth cylinder void will be carefully lit to create a spectacular space (far right).

One unit pops out
trees
Roof garden
link walkways every 3-4 floors
Entrance through Courtyard garden
Posh restaurant

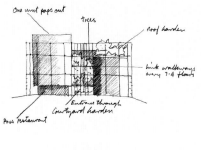
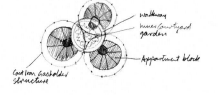

walkway
inner courtyard garden
Apartment block
Cast Iron Gasholder structure

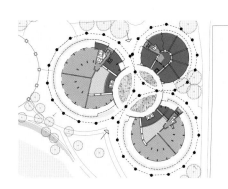

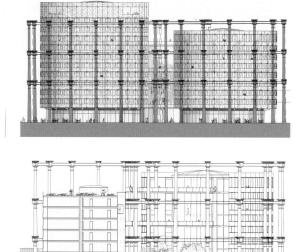

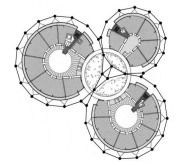

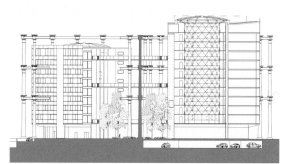

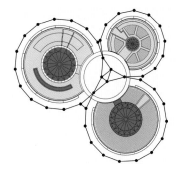

Detailed drawings of the design proposal show that the apartment layouts work well within the circular form of the enclosures. Each room is wedge-shaped with the broader face opening on to the outside view. On the inside, the apartments are accessed from a walkway which opens on to a central glazed atrium space. The vertical circulation cores for each block are connected at every 4th floor level by a communal walkway which circumvents the central cylindrical void space (left). The relocation of the gas holders closer to the Regents Canal provides a waterside setting for residents (right).

Mary Rose Museum Portsmouth, UK, concept stage

The Mary Rose was the pride of King Henry VIII's navy, the flagship of the Royal High Admiral and one of the first ships in the world to have gunports so that it could fire broadsides. It was a national tragedy when, after some 34 years of service, the carrack suddenly rolled over after an affray with the French fleet on 18 July 1545. (It is thought that the badly trained crew failed to close the lower gunports after the action.) The ship sank to the bottom of the Solent and remained there partly entombed in mud until its remains were brought to the surface in October 1982. The starboard side of the ship was preserved by being covered by ooze, and so were 19,000 objects ranging from the great cannons to needles and combs.

The remains were taken to Portsmouth Historic Dockyard and placed in an existing dry dock, adjacent to the one occupied by Nelson's flagship Victory. A temporary enclosure was made round the ship to allow the gradual process of preserving the timbers by dehydrating them very slowly; the objects found with it were housed in a Georgian naval warehouse 300m away.

Working with exhibition designers Land Design Studio and interior architects Pringle Brandon, Wilkinson Eyre evolved the dramatic notion of replacing the lost half of the ship with a glass analogue in which the public can wander to look at the preserved timbers and examine many of the artefacts in sealed transparent capsules located roughly where the objects would have been used when the ship was in service. The preserved side of the Mary Rose is of course the main exhibit, but it will be contained in its "hotbox" in which it is to remain sealed until conservation of the timber is complete. When the drying process is finished, the hotbox will be removed and the two halves of the ship, real and virtual, timber and transparent, will be united visually, so visitors will be able to look directly from the new glass galleries into the original decks they echo.

Chris Wilkinson: The remains of the hull, still in the process of preservation in the dry dock since they were brought to the surface in 1982, form the primary basis for the new museum. First impressions of the solidity of the rich bulky timbers bolted together in a carvel system are misleading. Even with the extensive preservation treatment, these timbers are incredibly vulnerable and need a carefully controlled environment (top right).

The architectural concept starts from the inside out, with the actual hull being supplemented with a "virtual hull" of glass construction. The two elements form a composition which gives an abstract impression of the original ship. In the central space attached to the virtual hull, three decks will be constructed which will house many of the original artefacts in their actual equivalent location, making it easier for visitors to piece together a more accurate idea of what life aboard the Tudor warship was like (main image and bottom).

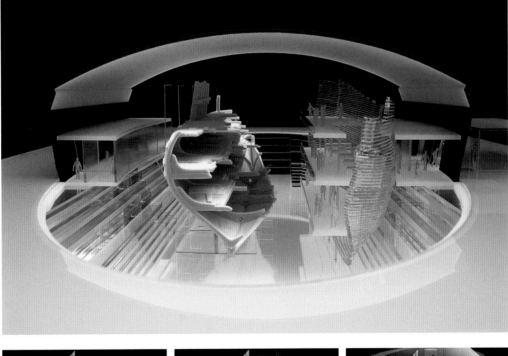

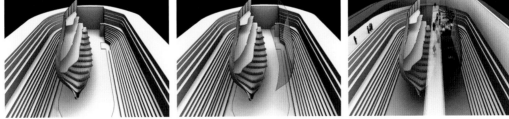

The hall that will cover all this (and the whole of the dry dock) is to be kept low and minimal in plan, so that it will not block views of the Victory—though its curving cladding will be of black planking in deference to the wooden walls of the heroic battleship. Seen from up on the deck of Nelson's flagship, the elliptical metal roof of the Mary Rose Museum will curve gently in two directions before forming a distinct eaves line following the ring beam round the circumference of the building. To minimise disruption to the Historic Dockyard, the parabolic roof structure will be prefabricated off-site in lightweight concrete and craned into position to act as the lid of what the architects call "a finely crafted wooden jewellery box." At the west end of the box, the wall will be fully glazed with a balcony that, like the adjacent Great Cabin of the Victory, will look out over the Historic Dockyard.

At first floor level, slot windows will sit behind black timber louvres. Their light will be carefully mixed with illumination from artificial sources designed to reveal the galleries and the great diversity of individual exhibits. Throughout the processes of construction and preservation, the public will be able to visit and see the remains of the great ship: a very difficult challenge in terms of temperature and humidity, careful control of which is vital to preserve the delicate exhibits.

The isometric shows how the building extends the form of the dry dock and provides a tight enclosure to the actual and virtual hulls. This central hall becomes an appropriately grand setting for the Mary Rose, but remains economical in terms of maintaining a strictly controlled environment (top left).

Within its sensitive context adjacent to the HMS Victory, the oval shape of the new museum, with its low profile domed roof, makes a gentle but positive contribution. Whilst its form alludes to naval design, it is clearly a piece of contemporary architecture and avoids pastiche (bottom).

The raked timber cladding, however, draws inspiration from the carvel construction of the original hull and bears inscriptions from the sailors' markings found on their belongings (middle right).

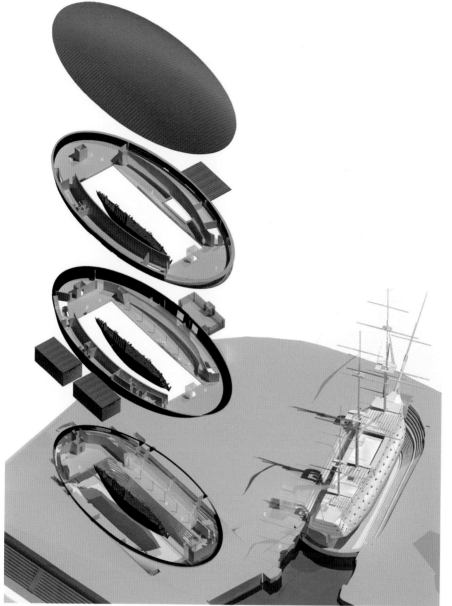

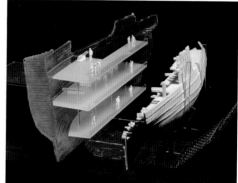

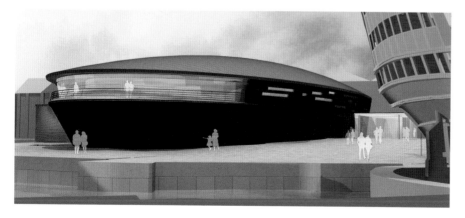

Energy for air conditioning will be generated in a remote existing boiler house, and the design team is exploring potential contributions from renewable resources. The jewel box will be airtight, and to help achieve the latter, visitors will enter the museum proper through a minimalist glass rectangular entrance pavilion which will formally complement the dark curvilinear box.

The Mary Rose Trust is working towards the £23 million needed to bring the wreck and its contents together under the shining shell, and now has collected enough to anticipate completion of the remarkable project in 2011, the 500th anniversary of the ship's first voyage.

The Mary Rose Trust (client); Davis Langdon; Gifford & Partners; Land Design Studio; Pringle Brandon

In terms of the architectural narrative, the mussel shell motif expresses the concept of a tight-fitting enclosure protecting precious contents (right).

Nesciobrug Amsterdam, The Netherlands, 2006

To deal with intense demand for housing in the Dutch capital, the IJburg district north of Amsterdam is being created on largely reclaimed land. Seven artificial islands are being made in the IJmeer, a freshwater lake created in the 1930s by closing a North Sea inlet. Over the years, the area has been colonised by wild species, so now it is a nature reserve, and a city quarter designed to cater for 45,000 people by 2012 is being added. It is essential that ecology and the new human habitats should not conflict, so great care is being taken to reconcile the two.

IJburg is connected to the main part of the city by tram and metro as well as a road, but another bridge over the Rijnkanaal was needed for cyclists and pedestrians who would otherwise be faced by a long and time-consuming detour. In the other direction, it has been a direct connection for the inhabitants of Amsterdam to the Diemerpark, one of the largest parks in the city and perhaps the major attraction of the new suburb.

Wilkinson Eyre have designed the new connection which was subject to a difficult range of conditions and constraints. Because of the busy shipping on the Rijnkanaal, the Nescio bridge had to have clearance of 10m over the water and a span of 163m; for the same reason, it had to be erectable with minimal disturbance. Because of the very special nature of the place, the link had to make as little visual impact as possible, so a cable-stayed bridge, for instance, was out of the question. Because the deck is so high up, much design effort has been expended in creating a fluid form that from underneath constitutes an arch across the water.

141

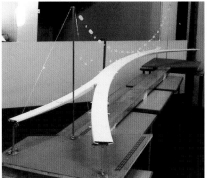

Jim Eyre: The intention here was to design a lightweight structure, stiff enough to be brought in one piece over the majority of the busy canal so as to minimise disruption (right).

Suspension bridges are notoriously sensitive to wind, and as such, long spans must be rigorously tested (left).

Working with Arup/Grontmij, Wilkinson Eyre decided to make a suspension bridge—curiously in a country full of bridges, the first one to be built in the Netherlands. A mono-cable system was chosen to support the steel box girder deck, a structure employed because the method of construction was stiff and light enough to allow the main span to be floated to position down the canal before being hoisted into place by floating cranes. The bridge is structurally symmetrical about the centre of the mid span, so that at any point, loads are carried from one side only by the cable and the hangers from the catenary cable. Very soft ground at each side of the site made essential two backstays to stabilise each mast and avoid large horizontal stresses in the foundations that are common in most suspension bridge constructions. Gently curved in plan to add stiffness to the deck and to follow natural desire lines, the bridge bifurcates at each end, so cyclists and pedestrians pass the masts on different sides. At both ends of the bridge, the backstays support the two branches of the deck. The pedestrian branches terminate in stairs, while the cycle ones are ramped as part of the concrete approach structures. The south ramp is stepped because of local topographical constraints (a steeper gradient than normal is required to avoid an existing house); on the north bank, the ramp forms a consistent sweep along the canal bank. Ramps and stairs are carefully landscaped to signal the routes and to act as transitional zones between canal banks and the bridge.

Nesciobrug, a dramatic, generous and elegant addition to the remarkable IJ landscape, opened in April 2006.

Project Bureau IJburg (client); Arup; Grontmij

Seen from below, the languid, flowing curves are evident, having been painstakingly refined on a 3D computer model to respond to the plan form and structural depth required. Curving planes create arrises which must not appear to abruptly change direction (top).

High over the Amsterdam-Rhine Canal the bridge provides a route which flows effortlessly from one neighbourhood (Diemen) to the new city quarter of IJburg (bottom).

145

Brighton Marina Brighton, UK, due for completion 2012

Brighton Marina, built in the 1960s, has never been satisfactorily related to the Regency resort either visually or physically. It was a daring proposal in its time, a large harbour on a shelterless shore—the biggest in Britain built out into the sea at the base of the white chalk cliffs. But several compromises had to be made to ensure economic viability, for instance the creation of big blind sheds for leisure functions and a dreary supermarket surrounded by surface level car parking to the west (city) end of the development. In 1996, the Brunswick Developments Group acquired a long lease on the marina from the city council and more recently decided to radically reorganise the west end of the complex. Wilkinson Eyre were asked to make a scheme that will act as a gateway to the city from the east and a landmark from both sea and city. The scheme will incorporate housing (of which 40% will be affordable flats), new public open spaces, restaurants and cafés.

147

Tall buildings are controversial in Brighton, because it is important to preserve the scale of the 19th century city and to safeguard the crest of the cliffs from visual intrusion. The new tower is deemed to be too far from the shore to interfere with the cliff line. In plan, it will be tapered towards the south both to emphasise its slenderness and to form a prow to face the sea. Above level 30, floor plates will be increasingly reduced and tapered to cut down the perceived mass against the sky. Vertical strips of balconies will contrast with white, slightly undulating imperforate strips of opaque glass to increase further the tower's impression of slimness. The top of the tower will have a public viewing gallery offering 360-degree views of sea, city, the cliffs and the Downs behind them.

On the south side of the platform below and projecting into the water, will be three residential buildings strung out along a new promenade of differing heights. On the other (north) side of the promenade will be a further string of residential buildings. The promenade will terminate on the West Quay of the inner harbour—the side of the marina itself. Two new buildings on the quay will have a range of different kinds of flats over a colonnade containing retail and catering uses, marine offices and the yacht club.

Jim Eyre: Aerial view with the development, which includes a 40-storey residential tower, located at the eastern end of the marina in front of the harbour entrance (centre).

A series of independent buildings are connected by a new deck, which is elevated so that views out of the marina can be enjoyed at the new street level. The potential of the waterfront location is realised by extending the inhabited frontage. The plan follows the water's edge and has eleven principal buildings (bottom).

Predominantly light in colour, curvilinear and playful, the forms draw on the Brighton tradition, transforming a hitherto lively but visually deficient and isolated city quarter (top).

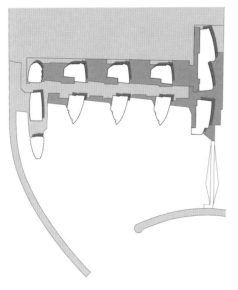

In general, the new buildings will be laid out to allow views of the sea, marina and city between and from them. A swing bridge is proposed across the mouth of the inner harbour. It will complete a continuous 2km pedestrian and cycle circuit round the marina. In addition, a new pedestrian bridge will be made between Black Rock Beach to the west of the site and the area north of the leisure buildings. At the moment, there is a partly underground connection that brings you out into the supermarket car park—a disagreeable route and an unpleasant destination. The two bridges, the restaurants and the viewing gallery should make the marina attractive to new sections of the public, and link the complex more effectively to Brighton and its beaches.

The site offers many possibilities for designing an environmentally responsible development, and a target has been set to reduce carbon emissions by 40% compared to a normal project of similar type and size. Another target is to generate 20% of renewable energy from solar, wind, wave and combined heat and power systems. Brighton's newest development could set a standard for the whole city, both in ecological and urban terms, for it is clearly a contemporary contribution to what *The Architectural Review* dubbed the "Nautical Tradition," which celebrates the qualities of seaside buildings, clear, fine-honed and daring in their response to the implacable forces of wind and waves.

Brunswick Developments Group/Barratt Southern Counties (client); Connell Mott MacDonald

Looking up at the main tower, the curved form is accentuated. Derived from a series of alternating sections of toroidal surfaces, the overall amplitude of the resulting vertical wave is actually quite small, but results in a dramatic white glass-clad form (left).

The tower is located at the southerly extreme of the marina to stand proud so that its full height can be seen and to distance itself from the cliffs behind and beyond the long views along the seafront (right).

Airports are always in flux. As demand grows, new routes are opened and aeroplanes get bigger, more and more gates are needed and new circulation patterns have to be evolved. They have to be capable of being created while normal business continues, so design has a major temporal component as well as functional and constructional ones. Gatwick, London's second international airport, grows as fast as any and change is often in jumps and leaps. The latest of these is a new link across one of the busiest plane taxiways to connect the North Terminal to a new satellite (Pier 6). A bridge was required to obviate 50,000 coach journeys a year across the taxiway between terminal and satellite.

Working with Arup, Wilkinson Eyre designed a bridge that could be prefabricated off-site and rapidly moved into position. Towers at either end contain vertical circulation and services. The bridge had to have a length of 198m and be high enough off the taxiway to allow a Boeing 747 to pass underneath; because of the size of future planes, the free span had to be 128m, and headroom above the taxiway had to be 22m. The main loads of the bridge are largely taken by two massive, three-dimensional Y-shaped props. Structurally, the bridge itself has a flat bottom chord fabricated from triangular steel components. Above, in the roof, two parallel steel trusses form the main compressive elements; they curve upwards towards the middle of the span to give the whole enough stiffness to deal with its long free span.

153

Jim Eyre: Assembled in the airport's apron, the fully clad bridge was rolled and lifted into place overnight in order not to close the busy taxiway (top left).

While the novelty evident in the flight crew's radio chatter may be wearing off, it remains a virtually unique and almost surreal experience to walk over moving aeroplanes (main image).

The bridge now provides a landmark for Gatwick Airport exceeded in height only by the control tower and visible from beyond the confines of the airport itself (bottom left).

The structure is completely contained within the cladding envelope, with glass walls inclining at 11 degrees outwards from floor to roof to facilitate views of the huge aircraft being slowly driven underneath, to reduce solar gain and obviate parallel reflections. The ceiling follows the structural curve of the roof and incorporates lighting, public address systems and two runs of chilled beams over continuous white acoustic rafts which, visually, are intended to evoke vapour trails.

The 2,700 ton bridge was prefabricated, clad and fitted with services and finishes at a special yard 1.5km from its final site and moved into position on its supports by two huge lifting towers. The whole operation took ten days. Only one bridge over an active taxiway has ever been built, at Denver in Colorado, where an 111m span connects two major elements of the complex. The new one at Gatwick is not only longer, but it stands out as a confident landmark among surrounding boxy buildings. Internally, its long views are free of the retail clutter that messes up most parts of large airports. At the same time, it offers passengers promenading to catch their planes a remarkable spatial experience in which they engage visually with the dramatic flux of systems and machines that will soon hurl them into the heavens.

BAA Gatwick (client); Arup; Mace; Pinniger & Partners

In section the requirement for two parallel routes is easily expressed—arrivals and departure. In order to maximise the openness on either side, the main spanning element is confined to a central spinal location (top).

Over the length of the bridge the structure must get deeper to facilitate the ability to span. The glazed enclosure follows to create a soaring space, free from the hectic activity of the terminal building (bottom).

Within, the result of the inclined planes and curving profiles allows the space to open out generously, perhaps giving a bit of lift to weary passengers and a prolonged view of aircraft to remind one that travel is still exciting (following pages).

157

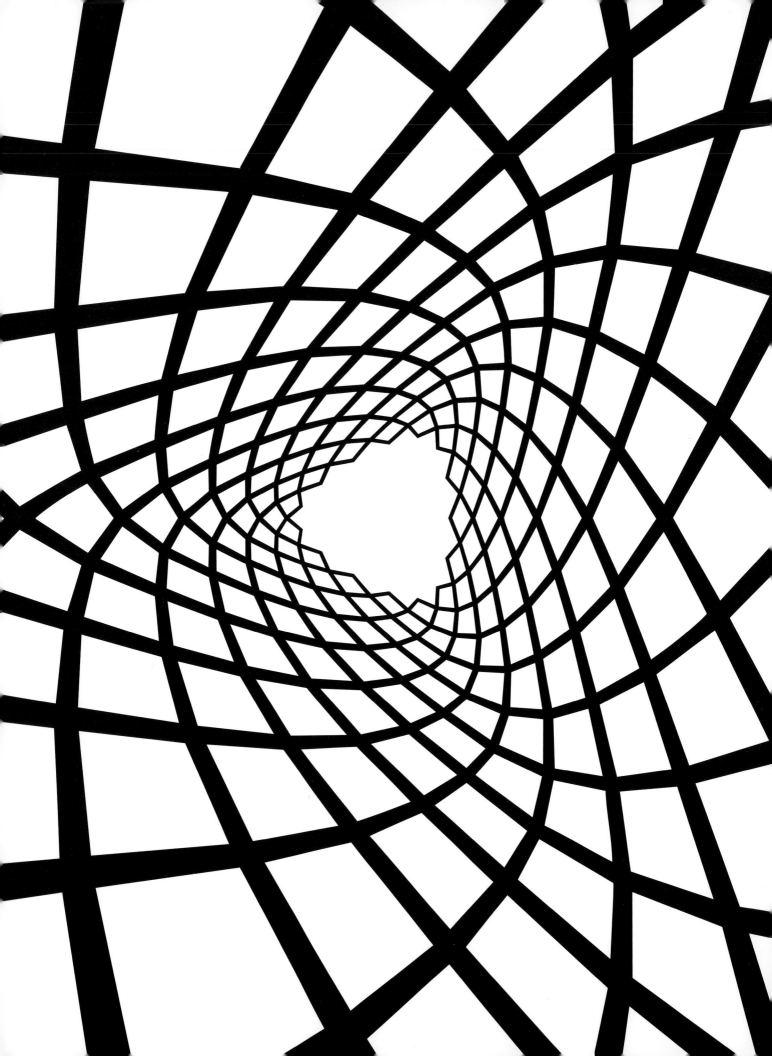

Guangzhou West Tower Guangzhou, China, 2009

Guangzhou is one of the wonder cities of China. It has a
three thousand year old trading history, and until the 19th
century, as Canton, it was virtually the only port in South
China open to foreign trade. Today, its economy, like that
of most of the south-east of China, is expanding at an
amazing rate, creating increasing demand for more and
bigger buildings. It will host the Asian Games in 2010 and
the authorities wanted a physical memorial to celebrate
the event. Wilkinson Eyre won an invited international
design competition for the landmark complex that will
become the icon of the city, like the Eiffel Tower or the
Sydney Opera house.

161

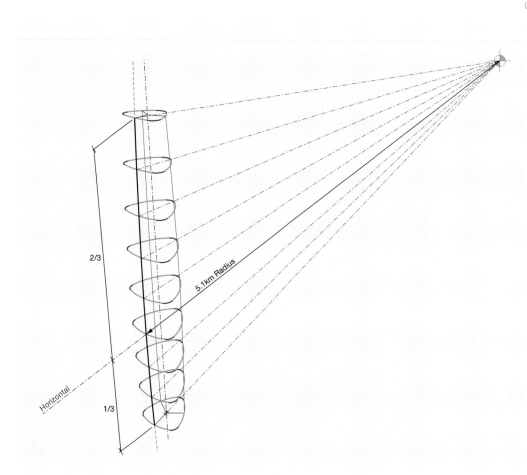

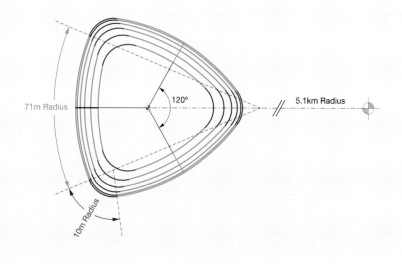

Chris Wilkinson: The apparently simple form of this building has only been achieved with the use of complex geometry. Each toroidal face is set out from a 5.1km radius, the centre of which, in the vertical axis, is offset below the midpoint of the tower to provide maximum girth to the offices on the 30th floor and a smaller floorplate to the upper levels. This geometry is resolved at the corners by the use of a simple repetitive radius of 10m swept down to round off where the adjoining toroidal surfaces would meet (left).

More complexity is revealed in the section, which shows the central space about the hotel lobby on the 70th floor opened up to create a spectacular atrium (far right).

The curved triangular plan proved to be an efficient layout, with a central triangular core. It offers easily divisible, flexible working space on three sides, with three access points to the core (bottom right).

On the upper floors, hotel rooms are arranged around the perimeter of the building to maximise views, and are accessed from an internal gallery looking into the atrium (top right).

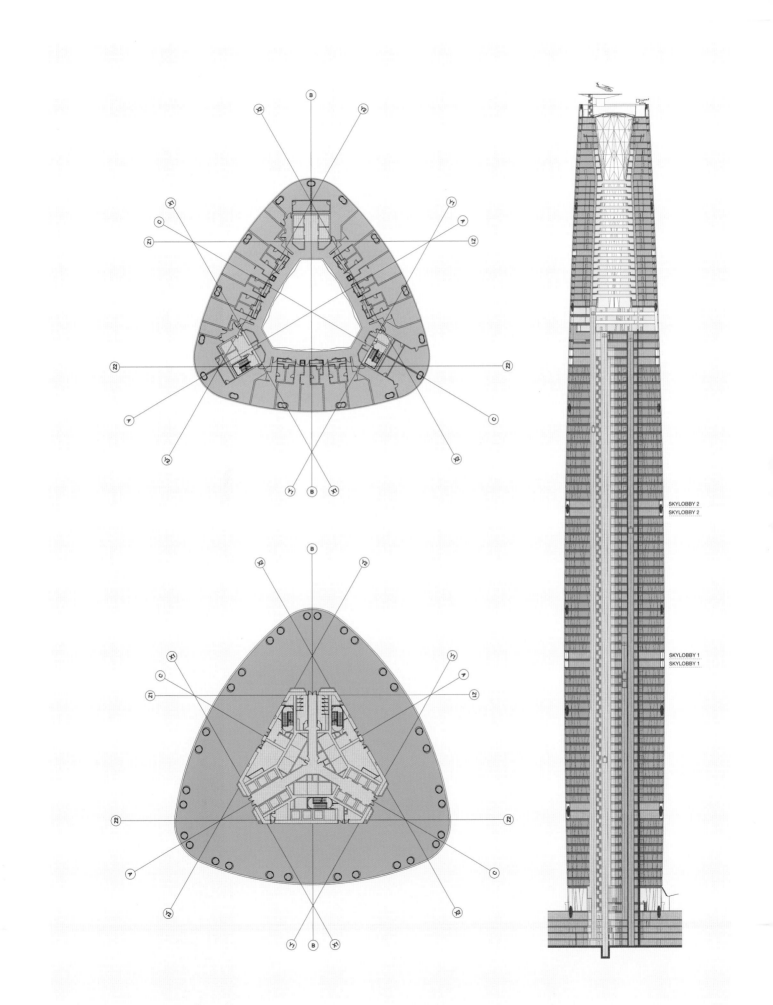

SKYLOBBY 2
SKYLOBBY 2

SKYLOBBY 1
SKYLOBBY 1

The brief required a mixed-use tower, intended to be the first of a pair. The lower 66 floors of the 437.5m high structure will provide 190,000m² of office space. Above, the upper 35 floors will be a remarkable luxury hotel, with its own ground floor entrance and separate lifts leading to a grand reception hall at the 70th level. A 32 floor high atrium open to the sky will bring air and light to the middle of the hotel plan and those of the 350 guest rooms that face into it. The tower will have 71 lifts, a swimming pool on the 69th level and refuge floors in case of fire. The apparently simple, elegant slim form is created with complex geometry. Each façade is a curved section of a toroid with a 5.1km radius set out asymmetrically to provide the maximum girth at a third of the height and the slimmest section at the top.

When the tower is joined by its twin, the two will frame Guangzhou Zhujiang New Town's main axis to connect the commercial district with the cultural quarter and the Pearl River to the south. At the base of the towers, low-level buildings will provide facilities like a conference centre for local business, and they will reinforce the streetscape and integrate the towers into the urban fabric. The towers will have their moment as the tallest in China, a record that will doubtlessly soon be broken, but there is much more to them than a vulgar race for height.

At competition stage, we explored options for the shape and structure of the tower with engineers Arup (top).

It was clear from the start that the special structural demands for a "supertower" would influence the architecture. Because of the height, there is a need for the external structure to cope with wind forces, and so the decision was made quite early on to design an exoskeletal frame with a slender aspect diamond pattern—the most efficient way of achieving the required combination of vertical and bracing loads. Each diamond extends through twelve floors to a height of 52m and the 'x' junctions extend through two floor levels. Two raking columns are shown here converging (bottom).

The external appearance of the tower is kept simple with a smooth skin of floor to ceiling glass with no spandrel panels. The plant room floors are expressed with louvred glass. The exoskeletal diamond structure can be seen behind the whole of the outer skin (far right).

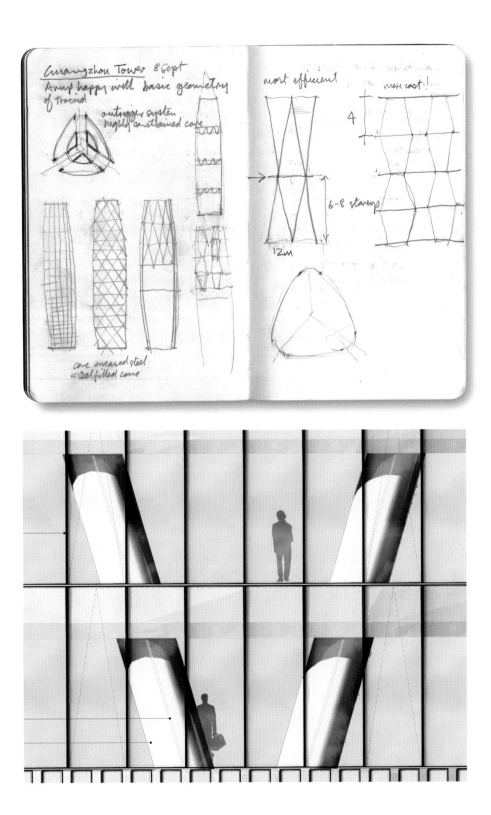

This model, made by Wilkinson Eyre for our 2005 "Reflections" exhibition at The Wapping Project in London, clearly shows the scale of the exoskeletal frame (left).

The shape of the internal atrium to the hotel floors tapers as it rises up, but then opens out again at the uppermost floors to create a kind of prismatic kaleidoscope which brings additional light into the space. This view looking up through the atrium reveals a diamond pattern overlaid onto the profiles of the internal balconies to reflect the external structure of the building (right).

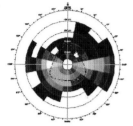
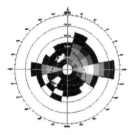
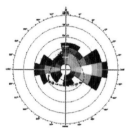
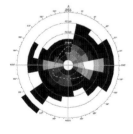

There are considerable environmental advantages to be derived from the triangular shape of the tower, which splits the wind smoothly on the corners to reduce downdraughts and can be oriented to reduce solar gain to the southern elevation. The optimum positioning for the tower was achieved through detailed wind analysis (far left).

The West Tower is placed on one side of Guangzhou Zhujiang New Town's main axis, and will be joined by a similar tower on the east side to complete the masterplan for this rapidly growing city (main image).

China's explosive growth is putting enormous pressure on the world's resources, and the architects (working with Arup as structural and environmental engineers) have attempted to create an environmentally efficient and flexible design. The rounded triangular plan of each tower is chosen to give a structure stiff against wind forces, and to generate efficient and flexible internal space-layouts. Loads are carried partly on the core and partly on the periphery in an expressed structural diagonal grid frame that has twelve-storey high rhomboidal elements (which are much more complicated to apply to a curved triangular plan than would appear at first). This giant rhombic pattern on the huge building will be clear for many miles, but it is modified at close range by a fenestration pattern that gives a more human scale. Scale will be further modulated by the double glass skin. It will have internal shading tuned to orientation that will form the main device for reducing solar gain, so each façade will have a subtly different inner pattern.

Work has already started on the first tower, and the pair is intended to be finished in time to make a dramatic urban gateway for the Games.

Guangzhou City Construction & Development Company (client); Arup; Lichtvision GmbH; South China Design Institute

Illustration credits

Airphotos/Gateshead Metropolitan Council: p. 39 · Arup:
p. 154 · Atelier Ten: p. 62 · BAA Aviation Photo Library:
p. 154 · Binet, Hélène: p. 32, 58, 64, 80, 81, 83, 85, 88, 89, 117 ·
Brittain, James: p. 12, 76, 80, 81, 83, 85, 86 · Collie, Keith/RIBA
Library Photographs Collection: p. 17 · Cook, Peter/VIEW:
p. 110/111 · Deacon, Richard/Tate Images, Courtesy of Lisson
Gallery, London: p. 11 · Dechau, Wilfried: p. 40, 42 · Deepres,
Ravi/BALTIC Centre for Contemporary Art: p. 23 · Drenth,
Alexandra: p. 144 · Firth, Ian/Flint and Neill Partnership:
p. 105 · Gilbert, Dennis/VIEW: p. 19, 31 · Glowfrog Studios:
p. 135 · GMJ Design: p. 131 · Guttridge, Nick: p. 64, 66, 67 ·
Halbe, Roland/RIBA Library Photographs Collection: p. 17 ·
Hall, Doug/Bonneys News Agency: p. 36, 39 · Hart, Rob't:
p. 142–143 · Hearn, Guy/Gateshead Metropolitan Borough
Council: p. 39 · Jefferson Air: p. 100 · Leaver, Ricky/Londonstills:
p. 126 · Luxmoore, Ben: p. 51, 54 · Magna: p. 54 · Mary Evans
Picture Library: p. 15 · Mary Rose Trust: p. 132, 135 · NMPFT
Daily Herald Archive/Science & Society Picture Library: p. 70 ·
NMPFT Kodak Collection/Science & Society Picture Library:
p. 15 · National Archive: p. 75 · Peacock, Graeme: p. 21, 29, 43 ·
Pepys Library, Magdalene College, Cambridge: p. 135 · Pinder,
Mark/Rex Features: p. 44 · Putler, Andrew: p. 118 · RIBA
Library Photographs Collection: p. 18 · Royal Botanic Gardens
Kew: p. 60, 64 · Simmons Aerofilms/Science & Society Picture
Library: p. 129 · Speirs and Major Associates: p. 9, 129 ·
Sternberg, Morley von: p. 9, 26, 51, 55, 57, 100–101 · Strachan,
Laurie/Alamy: p. 139 · Sumner, Edmund/VIEW: p. 26, 32, 48,
54, 55, 57, 106 · Tunick, Spencer: NewcastleGateshead 3,
Courtesy of Hales Gallery, London and I-20 Gallery, New
York: p. 45 · Wood, Nick: p. 47, 102, 108, 109, 152, 154–155,
156, 158/159 · All other images © Wilkinson Eyre Architects

List of staff

Thank you to: Shade Abdul, Ben Addy, Laufey Agnarsdottir, Matthew Appleton, Dimitros Argyros, Peter Ayres, Paul Baker, Sarah Ball, Dominic Balmforth, Eva Baranyai, Helen Barratt, Marc Barron, Timothy Barwell, Sophie Beard, Tom Bell, Anna Bergbom, Nathalie Bergvall, Dominic Bettison, Benjamin Bisek, Jelena Blazek, Yacine Bouzida, Dan Brill, Keith Brownlie, Leigh Bullimore, Christoph Burkhardt, Janna Bystrykh, Lauren Camberg, Rhys Cannon, Susan Carruth, Carlo Castelli, Ivy Chan, Gary Chapman, Samantha Chapman, Richard Cheesman, William Hailiang Chen, Katya Chikayer, Sam Chong, Gabrielle Code, Paul Conibere, John Coop, Grace Cooper, Joanne Cooper, Rose Courie, Sally Cowell, Isobel Cowen, Carin Crause, Stafford Critchlow, Ruth Cuenca, Louisa Cunningham, Ed Daines, Chris Davies, Katie Davies, Rebecca Davies, Simon Davis, James Daykin, Michael Dean, Andrew Demetrius, Olaf Detering, David Dickson, Ralph Dirkmann, Peter Dixon, Chris Donoghue, Brian Duffy, Thomas Dunn, Charles Dymond, Helen Eger, Christian Ernst, Mark Exon, Jim Eyre, Peter Feldmann, Hugh Fernando, Daniela Fogasova, Tim Francis, Christian Froggatt, Matthias Fruntke, Charles Gagnon, Gareth Gazey, Marco Gelsomini, Anneli Giencke, Graham Gilmour, Leigh Gittings, Robert Gluckman, Julia Glynn Smith, Simon Goldstein, Kate Gooch, Tom Goodall, Marta Goodrich, George Romanos Gortsios, Ford Graham, Vivienne Greenaway, Charlotte Griffiths, Damian Groves, Chris Hardie, Ed Harris, Robert Haworth, Jonathan Head, Magnus Hierta, Deborah Hobbs, Jordan Hodgson, Courtenay Holden, Ed Holloway, Gethin Hooper, Oliver Houchell, Clemence Huang, Elizabeth Hughes, Nanette Jackowski, Leif Johannsen, Masaki Kaizoe, Chikako Kanamoto, Nathaniel Keast, Emma Keyte, Martin Knight, Fruszina Korosy, Mimis Koumantanos, Carin Krause, Alex Kyriakides, Adrian Lai, Bosco Lam, Anne Langer, Jeffrey Lee, Richard Lee, Elisa Lei, Felix Lewis, Min Li, Huai Zhu Lim, James Llewellyn,

174

Christopher Lottersberger, Ruth Lucchini, Massimo Mantoan, James Marks, Leszek Marszalek, Giles Martin, Adam Matthews, Alex McAslan, Tim McDowell, Lila McFarlane, Frances McGeown, Stewart McGill, Nick McGough, Dominic McKenzie, Will McLardy, Kay McLean, Laura Mickleburgh, Philippe Monjaret, Oliver Moore, Tim Murray, Tony Musson, Katie Newall, Richard Noble, Hannah Nyman, Luke Olsen, Daniel Parker, James Parkin, Rita Patel, Vinod Patel, Lucy Paterson Holt, Romed Perfler, Robin Phillips, Toumas Pirinen, Susi Platt, Brian Poon, Suzaan Potgieter, Matthew Potter, Chris Poulton, Gideon Purser, Erik Ramelow, Helen Ramsden, Alexa Ratzlaff, Luis Reis, Cannon Rhys, Sebastien Ricard, Damon Richardson, Hugh Richardson, Luke Richardson, Thomas Rigby, Stefan Robanus, Simon Roberts, Alison Rolph, Melany Schaer, Pascale Scheurer, Annika Schollin, Andrea Seegers, John Smart, Catherine Smith, Vanessa Stacy, Ivan Subanovic, Mark Summerfield, Helen Summers, Franc Sumner, Amin Taha, Armelle Tardiveau, Christine Taylor, Neil Taylor, Erik Tellander, Clinton Terry, Paul Thompson, David Tigg, Simon Tonks, Van Tran, Charis Tsang, Alexandra Tsimperi, Adam Tucker, Geoff Turner, Lee Turner, Oliver Tyler, Silvia Ullmayer, Lindsey Urquhart, Natalie Urquhart, Filipa Valente, Laura Valverde, Sophie van Puyvelde, Naomi Vaughan, Karin Venter, Simon Vickers, Katharina von der Malsburg, Annette von Hagen, Walter Wang, Jan Warren, Camiel Weijenberg, Dan Welham, James White, Camilla Whitehead, Chris Wilkinson, Zoe Wilkinson, Lucy Wood, Anna Woodeson, James Woodhouse, Sam Wright, Oshri Yaniv, Tumpa Yasmin

Acknowledgements

This is our second book, covering the work of the practice since the year 2000. Over this period our architecture has evolved significantly. We feel that it continues to be distinguished by a willingness to adapt, exploring the boundaries between creative and scientific territories yet remaining specific to site and context.

The book represents a review of the fruits of many hours work over the last six years by all the architects and support staff at Wilkinson Eyre Architects, listed by name on the preceding pages, to whom we are eternally grateful. Of these, we would especially like to thank Emma Keyte for managing the project, and all those who have assisted in preparing the visual material.

We feel privileged to include the text and essays by Peter Davey and Kurt W. Forster, which are beautifully written and offer two different perspectives on our work. These are full of delights and surprises which are a pleasure to read.

For us, the design of the book is of the utmost importance, and we are thrilled with the work of Richard Smith and his colleagues at Jannuzzi Smith. Their approach has been creative and intellectually tireless in its execution, and we thank them for the beautiful results of their labour.

We would also like to thank our editor Henriette Mueller-Stahl and the team at Birkhäuser, who have been so supportive and enthusiastic throughout the project.

Finally, good architecture only exists where there are good clients and consultants, and we would like to thank all of the organisations and individuals we have worked with over the years.

Chris Wilkinson, Jim Eyre, Paul Baker, Keith Brownlie, Oliver Tyler, Stafford Critchlow and Dominic Bettison (Directors)